THERE WERE

Audrey Stepanian

Cover design by Katie Donlon

PAGE PUBLISHING, INC.
Conneaut Lake, PA

First originally published by Page Publishing 2021

ISBN 978-1-6624-4847-8 (pbk)
ISBN 978-1-6624-2640-7 (hc)
ISBN 978-1-6624-2639-1 (digital)

Printed in the United States of America

PREFACE

Let the redeemed of the Lord tell their story.

—Psalm 107:2

As the morning light dawned, I rose and opened the blind. During the night, we had gotten the first snowfall of the winter. As I peered out on all the beauty, I was lost for words to describe the sight before me. The richness of diamonds sparkled everywhere as the sun kissed the moisture pearls. The fluffy snow had wrapped the trees in garments of pure white. The branches of the trees were held up like angel wings.

In awe, I thought, *What a great God we have.* He gave us His Son to die on a cross. If we invite Him into our hearts to be our Savior, He wraps us in a pure white garment. Our face can now sparkle, as His Son fills our hearts with hope, promise, and love. Our arms can rise in prayer and praise like the wings of the angels.

> Sovereign God, at times it's easy to feel unsure of
> myself,
> Especially in situations where challenges feel like
> giants. Help me to trust that
> You've given me just what I need. You've crafted
> my life's story. (Taken from *Our Daily Bread
> Devotional*)

I am eighty-three years old. Many friends, who have known me through the years, have encouraged me with their words, "You have a story. You should write a book." About the time I would push the thought aside as being crazy, along would come another one saying, "You should write a book!" Through their encouragement, the Lord has gotten my attention, and so, with his guidance, I have done so. I dedicate this writing to my Lord for His glory. God bless you as you read.

INTRODUCTION

After Mom and Dad's passing, I found that Mom had written down some very interesting material. It told the beginning of my story. It told about that special day that they met and fell in love. How Mom left school to be married to Dad at sixteen years of age and Dad only being nineteen. Back in those days of the 1920s, that's just how things were. It tells of the beginning of a love story and how it endured through many hardships and the birth of eleven children.

May my writing do it justice!

THE BEGINNING

It was in the summer of 1925, the day of the Stiles family reunion. My mom-to-be, Mildred Harrington, was sitting in the back seat of a car visiting with her friends, laughing and anticipating the first day of school in the coming fall. Mom was fifteen. Another car pulled up close beside them. A young man named Melvin Bliss, my dad-to-be, was with his older cousin Jesse Baker and his girlfriend, Anna.

Melvin asked Mildred to go for a ride with them. Mildred was having such an enjoyable time with the girls that she almost declined. In the end, she did accept his invitation. During the ride, Melvin put his arm up on the seat behind Mildred. Mildred shared that during the ride, her whole world changed. She was in love with Melvin.

That very evening, they went on a moonlight drive to town for ice cream. As a fifteen-year-old, Mom was an attractive young lady at her best! Her long dark curly hair must have pleased my dad. Dad had bright blue eyes that sparkled. He also was always well dressed and behaved as a gentleman with good manners. On the way home, Melvin pulled the car off the road, stopping by a cornfield, across the road from the old fairgrounds. It was there that they shared their first kiss. Love was happening!

What an exciting day that must have been for both of them! They were probably very anxious for the next time they could spend time together, discovering new things about each other. When one is in love, suddenly the sky is bluer, the trees are greener, and the flowers radiate with color and beauty.

After the reunion and meeting Melvin, Mom attended school one more year to obtain all the credits she could. She took a heavier study plan to get more schooling before leaving to be married. For my father, it was back to work to save for the time when they could finally have the wedding. They made their plans when to marry after Dad's talk with her father. Dad's birthday was in December, and he desired to turn nineteen before marriage. Likewise, Mom wanted to be sixteen.

In the months that followed, their relationship blossomed. Melvin had a private conference with Mildred's dad, Grandpa Harrington. He gave his permission, and in December, Mildred and Melvin were wed at the pastor's home in Jasper, New York. Mom was just sixteen, and Dad was nineteen. Through happy and hard times, their union produced eleven children and would last nearly fifty-nine years. Happy they were and so in love!

My mom was Mildred Irene Bliss, 1910–2006, a farmer's wife who raised a family of eleven children. In her retirement years, she served as the Troupsburg Town historian.

From her written words of memories in 1926,

> The hill road was almost impassable. In fact, we had to circle the "Little Woods" and come up by the field in the Model T and then walk part of the way to reach the white house on the hill. It was getting shady by then. The sun had been bright and the sky very blue all day although it was very cold, and by nightfall, it would be zero at least.
>
> On December 18, 1926, we ate lunch, and then with my mom accompanying us, we drove to Jasper, where the marriage ceremony was performed by the Rev. Helena Chaplin in the Methodist parsonage. With no blood test required, the license had been procured at the town clerk's office with both of our parents signing. Christmas was only one week away, so we all went to Hornell to do our shopping in one of the following days that week.
>
> The following week, news was out that we were married. Some of the neighbors planned a shower for us, and they came to my parents'

house (where we were staying and going to live) on New Year's Eve, either by sleigh or walking up the hill. What fun that brought to our new home!

The following week, a large woodpile was buzzed up, and a good lot of it taken to the village of Troupsburg, where my mom and dad and my three brothers were moving. They had rented the house by the ME Church. At that time, a wood furnace and a big cookstove in the kitchen were the heat and cooking with no electricity. There was a barn nearby, so they took two cows with them, and others in town were happy to buy the extra milk by the quart.

Back on the farm, we made a trip to a secondhand furniture store in Hornell and purchased a nice used dresser, a round top table, and a library table. Six kitchen chairs and two rockers from Griggs Furniture Store in Troupsburg were also purchased. Each family gave us a bed, and we bought a used wood heater, which worked well, and our Kalamazoo kitchen range came after three or four weeks of waiting.

Melvin owned three cows, which he moved over to add to the ten cows that my dad had left on the farm. The milk was taken to the milk plant in town. One-half of the check was our income. We didn't have a car...so when it was our turn to take the milk to the plant (he changed with three other neighbors), I usually rode along in the horse-drawn sleigh and often spent the day with my mom in town. In the spring, we got a used Model T from Ervie Austin, and Dad started doing carpentry work.

As Told by Audrey

$\mathcal{D}$ad (Melvin) was a good carpenter and helped repair many things to bring in extra income. Owning a car working out was much more possible. Through the years, he not only built our new home with mom and the sons' help but built a house in Elkland, Pennsylvania, and one in Wellsville for his cousin.

During their early days of marriage, Mom (Mildred) wrote how they spent some evenings practicing their music. Dad had a guitar and was good on the harmonica and later the violin. Mom played chords on the old upright piano given to them by her parents. In those days, there were no electric lights, radio, or television, so they relied on family and friends for entertainment.

In later days, Mom and Dad mentioned many times how they attended the fairs held at the old fairgrounds, which were located just a short distance from where they now lived. It must have been a happy gathering place for many.

The following year, Mom and Dad decided to move to the Bliss Homestead as his father and mother were getting too old to work the farm. Mom and Dad moved there and purchased the homestead by giving up one-half of their milk check to his parents for them to live on. In December the following year, they moved all their household goods onto a lumber wagon and a Model T Ford and traveled over frozen and muddy roads to the original Bliss homestead in the area of Young Hickory in Troupsburg, New York. They settled into their home as they awaited the arrival of their first child. January brought somewhat warmer temperatures with clouds, rain, and more mud.

My parents once told me that they never accepted or asked for welfare. When they were starting out, buying Grandpa Bliss's farm, they put in an extra acre or two of potatoes as a cash crop to sell to bring in extra money to care for themselves.

Sharing the milk check was not always easy for the parents or Mom and Dad. One July, their check from nineteen cows was only sixty-six dollars to be shared. They owned many chickens and grew most of their food. Beyond that, they did without. Dad was not always paid in cash. One time, his pay was a topcoat with a fur collar and another time, a violin! He was very pleased to get them!

I once heard a minister preach a sermon that I never forgot. The subject being "What is that in your hand?" What do you have that you can fill the need with, or what ability or talent do you possess to be able to meet this need? I know this way of thinking helped my family and certainly me to be independent, willing to work, and know that needs would be supplied by the hand of the Lord. We were helped. We were shown. We were blessed!

> For I am the Lord, your God who takes hold of
> your right hand and says to you,
> Do not fear; I will help you. (Isa. 41:13)

DURING THE DEPRESSION

How was it for Mom and Dad during the Depression? They didn't notice much being different, except for lack of cash. Dad had a silver dollar, which he desired to keep. I never knew just why it was so special. Maybe his father had given it to him, or it may have been very old. Out of necessity, he had to part with it to buy a fifty-pound bag of flour. The flour came in a cotton knit flowered bag. Mom made new underwear from the bag. Until her birthday, she only owned one dress. Uncle Dorr was working for them, and from his wages, he bought material for her to make a dress. They surely were poor for Mom to sew undies out of a flour sack and how special it was for her brother to provide the fabric to sew a new dress as a present. Doing without is hard, but it brings out the best in people on many occasions.

Other people had it much worse. They lost everything they had and were forced to stand in bread lines to eat. Farmers had good food.

MOM'S BROTHER

Uncle Craig Harrington

(As Written by My Sister-in-Law Carol)

Carol interviewed Uncle Craig for an assignment for one of her college courses. I love these two stories and Uncle Craig's picture; therefore, I cannot leave them out! Carol (the writer) has passed away with cancer. She wrote a book but did not have it published, so including this as my remembrance of her.

Uncle Craig was a gentle soul and loved by our family. He never graduated from high school or married. My brother Melvin Jr. and Carol were visiting him at his home one day, and Carol wrote down what she heard as Uncle Craig shared these two recollections with them word for word.

As Told by Uncle Craig
Harrington to Melvin Jr.

May 1945

Beautiful day, 'bout like yesterday. Come a big blow and took a bunch of that tin off the roof over the living room. Boards under the tin were three inches apart, had to fill in the spaces, put on asphalt shingles. Made a wavy roof, didn't work too good. Decided that while the roof was off to put in that little dormer that faced Brother Roy's. Remember that? Anyway, we lacked a pine board to finish up the trim so I went to Melvin's to get it.

Your mother was still in bed from having you. You was two days old and lyin' there all curled up. That was the first time I saw you.

Next day, I started dragging. We had just got that H-tractor, and I was anxious to try it out. Made a couple of trips around the field and had to do chores. Next morning, it had snowed. Didn't get back to that field for three weeks.

'Twas a good year for maple syrup. The sugar bush was in the gully, where all them limby maples was. Gotta have limby trees to get lots of sap. Take a good shade tree, you can pret'near hang buckets all around.

Uncle Craig's Story
about the Maytag

(Another Story about My Grandparents Told by Uncle Craig)

In 1917, Dad bought the—place. He traded a big black cow that come with the farm for a wooden tub motorized Maytag washer—had an engine you had to mix gas and oil for like a chain saw. Before you started it, you had to open the kitchen window and run the metal exhaust hose outside. Well, whenever that thing started up (it had a pedal you kicked to start it), it sputtered and coughed out black smoke, and sometimes it would quit in the middle of a wash.

I used to hate Mondays. Uncle George was livin' with us and Grampa, most of the time, so there my mother was with a house full of menfolk to cook for and that washer to put up with. She'd be mad all day at everybody.

She finally traded the washer to a couple of newlyweds for a Victrola. I remember the day they come in their Model-A Roadster with the Victrola loaded in the boot. They got that thing out without a scratch, loaded up that washing machine, and off it went. That big black cow was worth more'n that washer and Victrola put together!

THE BIRTHS OF EACH CHILD

(In Mom's Writing I Found Details about Each Birth)

*I*n mid-January, it became apparent that the baby was arriving soon. Dr. Clark and midwife came calling at 9:00 p.m. Soon after midnight the next day in 1928, their first son, Larry, arrived. The proud new father was delegated the job of emptying the pans of dirty water outside. He was slow to return as he fainted and cut his face on the frozen ground. Others never allowed him to forget that. A familiar expression at the time was "Soft as gopher feathers." Baby Larry was nicknamed "Gopher." By the time he was high-chair age, the proud father was saying, "Gopher's going to college," implying he was too smart to spend his life working as hard as his dad had.

A daughter was born next the following November 1929. Betty was a beautiful small baby. She did not have much hair but was cherished and well-gifted by both sets of grandparents. Earl, the second son, arrived 11:45 p.m. in July 1932. Mom had figured he would be born a day later, but she was off by fifteen minutes. He was a heavy bundle, so Mom was glad to carry him in a new position. There was a short thunderstorm during his delivery. By September 1934, son Roy arrived. He grew into a strapping tall fellow of six feet four and wore a large shoe size. By spring, Mom and all four children caught the red measles. The two grandmas and Dad's sisters Delcie and Mollie all came to help during that time.

In May 1936, Mom's doctor, Dr. Clark, died. Dr. MacDonald was called to deliver me (Audrey) at four o'clock on a June afternoon. My Uncle Dorr's wife, Aunt Adah, came up to help, and the doctor handed me right to her. She and Uncle Dorr were always good to me and treated me special. I was a thin child with blue eyes and straight white-blond corn silk hair.

Along came another brother, Arling, in February 1939. He was born at the local hospital in Hornell. The reason he was not born at home was because Mom developed phlebitis, thus keeping her in bed for quite a spell. In June 1939 when the school closed, all six children came down with whooping cough. It was a very dry year with lots of grasshoppers. Dad had a tractor and threshing machine by now, so he went from farm to farm to harvest the grain for winter and extra income.

Bill joined our family in August 1941. He grew up to be very handsome like his Grandpa Harrington. Judy arrived in June 1943. The doctor had a flat tire on the way to deliver Judy,

Thus, she arrived before the doctor. She turned in to a cutie with long blond natural curls.

Melvin Jr. was born in May 1945. Another handsome blond.

Brother Alan arrived in June 1947. He was good in sports, loved them, and memorized all the scores. Mom desired just one more baby. Dad wasn't so sure it was a good idea. In September 1952, Bonnie arrived with her big dimples and happy smile. How they enjoyed her.

The first eight were born at home and the last three at the hospital. There were diapers hanging on the clothesline for twenty-five years straight, but the family was complete with seven boys and four girls!

My Memories of Growing Up on the Farm

I was born fifth in line in the Bliss family of eleven children. As a four- or five-year-old girl, I can picture myself on a quiet dirt road. On a slight bank stood a weatherworn two-story house we called home. The barn sat across the road. I don't remember much about that barn, only about the house where I lived with Dad, Mom, my big sister, and five brothers.

The large kitchen housed the woodstove, where all the wonderful aromas came from. Mom was a fantastic cook who never owned a cookbook. A dash of this and a coffee cup of that, she cooked from sense and feel. Farm fresh eggs and milk and garden vegetables canned and brought up from the cellar were staples in her recipes.

Off the kitchen was the old woodshed with our wood supply for heating. It was there that Dad would hang the butchered animals to freeze during a cold winter month. Eventually, the meat would be cut and canned for future nourishment and pleasure.

Next to the kitchen was a doorway, leading to a middle room of the house. I remember Mom coming home from the dentist, where she stood by the round woodstove warming herself. A trip to the dentist these days meant getting teeth pulled, not repaired. She was very quiet on that day.

The stairway to the upstairs led up from the middle room near the old woodstove. There was another room on the ground level— my parents' bedroom. It was there I lay so ill with pneumonia on an army cot. I don't remember much about the illness, except I faded in and out, and eventually, I was a well person again. Dr. MacDonald would come to our home when called. He tried a new drug that was discovered at about the time of my illness. It was called Sulfa. It worked very well and saved my life. This was the spring of 1942.

As I ascended the stairway in the middle room to the upstairs, I entered a bedroom that I shared with my older sister, Betty. It was very warm and snug as the chimney extended up through the room. As I passed on through our room, I entered another large room. Here were two double-sized metal beds made up with homemade quilts. These quilts were made with leftover material scraps and cotton flannel linings. This was the boys' room.

My mind's house tour takes me to a particular day in springtime. I was five years old and home from school, still recovering from pneumonia, and we had just finished lunch. I remember following Dad up the stairway leading to my bedroom. He checked the chimney, and we both came back down. This was the last time I was in that house.

He immediately called for help. The house was on fire! If there was a fire company in those days, it was poorly manned and equipped. Word spread quickly about the fire, and people soon arrived. They started carrying out what they could. They saved the upright piano and the old kitchen cabinet among other things. In her panic, Mom tried to save an enameled basin of milk, probably thinking she needed to save the milk for her children. By the time the other children arrived home on the school bus, the house had burned to the ground. Other than what they carried out, it was a total loss. Even the basin of milk was covered with soot. Nothing of our clothing and personal belongings were able to be saved as the fire engulfed the house so quickly, and the water supply was not adequate.

All the children had been born in that house, except Arling, Alan, and Bonnie. During each of Mom's home deliveries, Dad called the doctor on the party phone line. The neighbors would "rubber," or listen in when the phone rang, so word traveled quickly. Dad would then go after one of his sisters to act as a nursemaid.

Mom, Dad, and the other children went to live at my grandparents' home for a short time. I went to live with my aunt Adah and uncle Dorr. In the next couple of weeks, my parents made plans to get us back home together again. Since the house was gone, what were the possibilities for quick housing? The answer was to be found in the granary, the extra building where farmers kept the grain harvested using Dad's threshing machine. They emptied the granary of the grain, put down stud flooring, covered it with linoleum, and made it into two rooms. That's where we lived until late August when the new house was ready enough for us to live in.

Living in the granary was rather like being on a long camping trip. We stayed and played outdoors, weather permitting, and the farmwork was right there with us. Relatives came to visit. We were together and safe. It was all right! Upon entering the door, we walked into the kitchen, which was furnished with a table and chairs, the cabinet saved from the fire, and a kerosene cooking stove with an oven. Near the entrance to the inner room was an army cot. It was here that my oldest brother, Larry, slept. The inner room was the bedroom. Here were two double metal beds and one twin-size bed. My older sister, Betty, and I slept in the twin bed. Earl, Roy, and Arling slept in one of the double beds, and baby brother Bill joined Mom and Dad in the other. Clothing and bedding came from the sharing hearts of many people. There were homemade quilts and wool olive-green army surplus blankets to warm us. The decor certainly was not lovely or color-coordinated, but we were in a survival mode, and it fulfilled the need. At night, we could hear mice scurrying about, and when it began to rain, we could hear a melody of pitter-pats on the tin roof that kept us dry. Later came the heavy pounding of a downpour.

Each morning, Dad would fill four large milk cans with water and line them up in our kitchen area. A water dipper was nearby. That was our water supply for the day.

That summer, my dad, mom, and older brothers worked hard building the new house. The fire insurance did not cover the higher costs of lumber, which was in short supply due to the Great Depression and our country's preparation for World War II. My older sister Betty became the chief cook at the seasoned age of twelve. We grew a large vegetable garden, which produced tomatoes, corn, yellow beans, cabbage, lettuce, peas, and potatoes. Up the road on the corner lot, we would fill our containers with red ripe wild strawberries and go to the Johnson lot for wild blackberries. Work was a-plenty, and all hands were busy. Even the younger ones helped. Life was not easy, but no one seemed to complain. We were together, and life went on.

By the return of cold weather, we were living in what seemed to be a grand, new home! We did not enjoy the comforts of a modern furnace, but a wood and coal-burning furnace took its place later on. A cooking range stood in the kitchen and a round potbelly stove in the living room. We were thankful that heat rises. That meant that the heat from downstairs rose the open stairway to our bedrooms. The short supply of money didn't allow for storm windows, so the frost gathered on the windowpanes.

Our new home was built across and down the road from the one that had burned. The smell of new lumber was everywhere. Mom used shellac to protect some of the new wood as the shellac dried quicker than varnish. With so many feet walking about, the shellac was put on while we were asleep. The living room had a matched tongue and groove hardwood floor. The kitchen and dining room had wide plank flooring covered in linoleum. Today, covering a floor like that would be a cardinal sin. The house had four bedrooms upstairs.

My bedroom was on the upper left and to the back. It was painted a restful pastel blue. The next-to-the-bottom step in the open stairway lifted and was the entrance into a storage cupboard, where what few toys we owned were stored.

In the living room stood a floor model Philco radio. I remember December 7 of that year, which became known as Pearl Harbor Day. After Dad left for work, the announcement by F. D. Roosevelt of the declaration of war against Japan and Germany came over that radio. The next spring, ration books were issued for gasoline, sugar, meat, and coffee. All items became scarce.

The announcement of the death of President Franklin Delano Roosevelt in 1945 came to us from that radio. Mom stayed up late on Saturday evenings to do her ironing and to mop the kitchen floor. She tuned into the Grand Ole Opry to enjoy while she worked. After evening chores were done, my younger brothers would pull in close to the radio to listen to *The Lone Ranger*. Their imaginations would have them riding the swift horses engaged in battle. We often played tricks on one another. During one of the *Lone Ranger* programs, an older brother walked up behind two of the younger ones, pointing his finger between their shoulders and yelling, "Stick 'em up!" They jumped from their chairs with hands held high!

I remember watching my brothers down on the floor building farms. They built fences with clothespins for posts and string for wire. They saved the string that came tied around packages of store-bought meat to purpose as wire. They usually had a small toy John Deere Tractor and cart, some cows, a couple of horses, sheep, and pigs. Some fences were made with small branches. No matter what, they had fun creating their farms!

Saturday night was bath night in a round metal tub near the kitchen range. Water was heated on the side reservoir of the woodstove, the teakettle, and large metal dishpans. The water was changed for every two children. The new house did have an inside flushing water closet rather than an outside privy. Our washings were done in the kitchen with the aid of our ringer washer. Two big tubs were filled with water for rinsing. The clean clothes were hung outside to dry. Mom took pride in hanging a clean white wash. During the winter, the clothing froze stiff. We took them from lines to the large clothes bars near the potbelly stove in the living room to dry. Steam irons had not been thought of yet. The starched shirts and blouses had to be sprinkled and rolled up to dampen. When ironed, the clothing looked crisp and smooth.

We did not own a refrigerator until I was in high school. We used the large gallon size jars that Hellmann's Mayonnaise originally came in for containers. We filled them with our milk supply and Jell-O or whatever needed to be kept cold. We submerged the sealed jars into the cold water inside our milk cooler in the milk house. When we needed something, we made a quick trip to get it. Not much was left over to refrigerate after mealtime, as there were so many hungry mouths to feed.

OLD REX

No farm was complete without a family dog. Old Rex was ours. He was a sweet-natured light-golden-brown retriever. Rex would usually be where the family was when he could be. Since Rex was an outside pet, he waited patiently at the back door. He knew when our mealtime was over, that his was soon to come. These were the days before dog food. He survived very well on the scraps and leftovers from our table. When the vet visited our farm to treat the sick cows, Rex was looked at, as he had need. Any shots that he needed were administered at the town fire hall.

When we played ball games in the yard, he was there. In the late afternoon, he answered to a whistle and accompanied the chosen one to go to the far lot and bring the cows in for the evening milking. While the milking was in progress, he waited at the edge of the barn floor near the milk house. At that time, milk cans with strainers were lined with flannel squares to collect and strain the milk before we placed it into the milk cooler. When the strainer was removed and rinsed for storing, the milk-soaked flannel square was to be thrown away. Rex always retrieved that and swallowed the whole thing in one gulp. No harm seemed to result from his unusual snacking habits as he lived to be an old dog. Many happy memories come to mind from having been raised in the country on our farm.

THE OLD OAK TABLE

I remember the round oak table. When it would get close to mealtime, we would take a head count and decide how many table leaves we would need to accommodate the people present. In those days, there were three full meals a day. I usually placed ten to twelve plates on the table.

Breakfast would consist of eggs, homegrown bacon or side pork, and either toast, pancakes, or muffins. If we had cereal, it was hot oatmeal or cold cornflakes and shredded wheat. The other meals consisted of a large kettle of homegrown potatoes, yellow beans, either canned or fresh from the garden, a head of fresh cabbage grated fine and made into a wonderful crunchy salad, and our farm meat. We enjoyed fresh sweet corn and sliced tomatoes when they were in season.

We had a good variety of meat. It would be fresh chicken, rabbit, or roast beef, fresh or canned, ground burgers, or sliced pork fried to a golden brown in the black iron skillets on the old woodstove. In November, during hunting season, we would enjoy pans of ground venison and onions made into patties. There was always plenty of gravy made from meat scraps and farm milk.

For dessert—to last for two meals—each forenoon, Mom and I would bake two pies and a large loaf cake. The icing for the cake didn't come from a plastic container but rather from the stovetop. Mom and I would boil sugar, Hershey's cocoa, and milk until they thickened. A lump of real butter and vanilla was added, and then the frosting was beaten by hand until it was thick and smooth—just the right consistency to spread on the warm yellow cake.

The pies were made with eggs and milk. The custard filling was poured into Mom's tender piecrust. Sometimes the pies were filled with apples from the orchard behind the house, or, with blackberries in season. The food was plain and simple, but we always seemed to have plenty. Many times, there would be extra visitors sharing our meals around the old oak table. During the Depression, relatives knew they could get a good meal on the farm with us. They would just show up and be fed.

In strawberry season, we would wait until the cool of the evening after milking was done, and with milk pails and berry buckets in hand, we would head for the strawberry patch and pick until dark. We never seemed to mind the work. Work turned to fun as we laughed and shared together, thinking about what was to come. Upon returning home, we would spread the waxed paper on the table. Each sitting at their designated place, we hulled the sweet-smelling berries. Soon, two big yellow Pyrex bowls would be heaped with red berries. Mom would fire up the woodstove to get the oven to the correct temperature. She would then stir the shortcake dough and bake it in round cake pans. While the dough baked, we would crush the berries with the hand potato masher. When they were just right, we would add just enough sugar to make the berries sweeter and juicy. Mom then spooned the berries over the warm cake. When the first layer was covered, on went another layer, with more berries and juice running down the sides. Sometimes we were able to save cream, skimmed from our milk cans. Whipped in soft peaks, it made a real treat on our shortcake. Now it was time! We would sit at the old oak table and feast on the fruit of our labor. We enjoyed conversation and playing cards—the old oak table being the centerpiece of much pleasure.

SLEDDING

What do families do for fun and entertainment on a farmstead back in the country in wintertime? We owned sleds! The neighbors had a toboggan. Occasionally, we would borrow it, and using the hill across the meadow in front of our farmhouse, we enjoyed many slides down the hill. The younger family members were intermingled with the older to distribute the weight and give a safer, faster ride. One big push, and down we'd go! The woods behind the house were filled with maple trees. We forged a trail, winding between the trees. The sleds sped swiftly down the steep incline. Over and over we would go until our feet and fingers were numb and stinging from the cold.

With snow-covered boots and clothing, we would head for the back room and the warmth of the kitchen range. A treat was soon to follow. Sometimes we cranked a freezer of homemade ice cream. Other times, we enjoyed popcorn balls, homemade chocolate fudge, or jack wax.

Now it was time for the boys to do the nighttime milking and for us to prepare the evening meal. The cold winter afternoon was now a happy memory.

CHRISTMAS

*M*om spoke in her early writing that shortly after getting married, they went to Hornell shopping a week before Christmas. That changed with the arrival of each child and as everyday pressures of life fell upon them.

I remember as a child watching down the road for their headlights to appear upon their return on Christmas Eve. They would also stop in town on their way home for the late arrival of packages that were ordered through the Montgomery Ward catalog. They managed to buy one gift for each child plus a large bowl of tangerines, walnuts in their shells, and ribbon candy mixture.

Our tree was freshly cut from the pine grove across the meadow in front of our home. We had a stand made in agriculture class at school. It was made out of a cinder block. We had one string of seven large lights. There were two yellow, two red, two green, and one white. We placed our homemade color chains on the tree, and Mom always bought a new box of icicles for glitter.

After the morning chores were done, we had a big breakfast together and then shared a gift for each person from under our tree. Following this, we all got neatly dressed, and by noon, we were at Granddad and Grandma Harrington's house for a wonderful feast of chicken, mashed potatoes, warm biscuits, and wonderful pies! By milking time, we were back home, and Christmas was a happy memory.

Now that I am older, I think back to those wonderful gatherings. There were so many of us and the rest of their family...nearly twenty people. Grandma worked so hard to make those times so very special for us.

When we would arrive, my grandparents would be right by the door to greet us and see what Santa had brought. Grandma had a huge cabbage salad ground fine topped with real Hellmann's Mayonnaise. How crunchy and good that was! There were homemade pies, pickles, jelly, and large cookie sheets full of hot biscuits. The chickens were raised on their farm. They had to be defeathered, cleaned, and cut up before the cooking process began. A lot of work!

Aunt Adah always brought at least three chickens, all cooked in abundant broth, ready to be browned down in the black skillets. Milk was added to the large broth kettle and thickened to be used on the mashed potatoes and warm biscuits. So much good food—everyone stuffed themselves. No one had to go without.

After the cleanup and the dishes were done, we gathered around their tree, finding a gift for everyone. Grandma sure could make it a special time for all.

A New Well

$\mathcal{M}$ost water supplies came from the springs on the hills. Our spring was running dry and needed to be replaced with a well. Three men and their big equipment arrived at our place. Today was the day, but Mom and Dad could not be home. My brother Earl was sick, and they were at the hospital with him. He ended up having an appendectomy.

In those times, with no nearby restaurants, working environments were obligated to provide meals. In Earl's absence, at twelve years old, I became the cook that day. I cooked the meat, a large kettle of potatoes, a dish of vegetables, and cabbage salad. We usually hand stirred a yellow loaf cake, frosted with our homemade boiled chocolate frosting. Served warm, these were very tasty. I don't remember if there was dessert that day, but my sister-in-law stopped in, just before mealtime, and helped to set the table. After the men were full, they reached into their pockets to get a dollar or two. Thinking she had prepared the meal, they offered Evelyn the money. She said, "No, Audrey cooked the meal!" I ended up with the money and lots of praise. Earl healed, and we had our new well.

They had to go to Bolivar to purchase the piping and all supplies necessary to finish the job. The new well was really needed. When the house burned, they lost everything for lack of a good water supply. They had learned the hard way the value of having a dependable water supply. The well turned out to be very deep and special, as you will see later in the story.

EVERY SEASON A REASON

Life was busy on the farm. Every season brought its own work. When the maple trees began to run, the trees were tapped and buckets hung. It was time to take the horse-drawn tub to the woods and collect the sap. We quickly moved from one bucket to the next, pouring the sap into the big horse-drawn wooden tub and headed for the sugarhouse. The fire was started under the long boiling pan, and sap was added and cooked down to syrup consistency. The maple syrup was strained, brought to a boil, poured into sterile jars, and sealed for future use. That sure tasted good on homemade sour milk pancakes with homegrown bacon. Mom always left a big yellow Pyrex bowl sitting out overnight so the milk would sour. In the morning, she stirred up the pancakes and baked them on the grill on the woodstove. The syrup could also be sold for needed extra cash.

Springtime brought forth the planting season. The plowing had been done in the fall. Now it was time to drag, fertilize, and plant the oats and field corn that would be used to feed the animals. The first cuttings of alfalfa were soon ready. Not far behind came haying time. It was cut, put in windrows, and then gathered with a pitchfork by hand into stacks. This was a hot job for everyone! The horse-drawn wagon would travel in and out of the rows. As it passed, the stacks of hay were pitched onto the wagons with forks. When the load was high and full, it was taken back to the barn to unload into the haymow. All day, it went back and forth, gathering hay for the winter.

Dad owned a threshing machine and traveled from farm to farm. All the neighbors gathered at each farm to share in the work, thus getting each one's crop harvested in turn. The farm wives knew about a day ahead when the thresher would be arriving at their place. They cleaned the house and baked pies. On the day of threshing, a big feast of meat, potatoes, cabbage salad, vegetables, homemade pickles, and hot biscuits with jelly were served, along with homemade pies. Cups were filled and refilled with good hot coffee.

After a hot meal to restore their energy, the farmers continued threshing and bagging the grain until milking time. Dirty and tired, they headed home to complete the evening milking.

Summers entailed long days of hard work. The cows had to be milked on schedule twice a day. They had to be fed grain also. Before we were able to own automated milkers, my brothers sat on a stool at each cow and hand-milked them. With twenty to twenty-five cows, that was a lot of hard work. Between milkings, the other work must be done. In the spring, crops had to be planted. The ground has to be plowed and dragged. Fertilizing is another need. As warmer weather arrives, the first cutting of alfalfa is ready. Then time to fill the hayloft with enough hay and straw for feeding and bedding for the winter. Threshing time comes so the grain is cut, and my father was busy arriving at each farm to thrash their grain for winter. The wives were busy canning for winter to keep all the hungry mouths fed. The garden had to be kept up with as the vegetables were ready to harvest. How delicious-tasting were the freshly picked tomatoes, new potatoes, and green peas. Best of all, don't forget the heaped plates of fresh sweet corn just picked before mealtime. We could eat to the fill. When the days' work was done and if time allowed, occasionally, we would attend a movie or have an evening game of baseball in our yard with four stones marking the bases. We would attend an occasional family reunion, and the month of August would bring a school bus trip to the county fair. It was hard to find time and energy for evening fun before nightfall, but all in all, it was a good life, a healthy and fulfilling life!

When fall arrived, the haymows and granaries were full of high-energy food to keep the animals wintered. Meanwhile, the wives were canning tomatoes, corn, peaches, wild berries, green and yellow beans, homemade jellies, and pickles to feed the families through the winter. The squash was gathered, and the apple, onion, and potato bins were filled also. Food was good, simple, and ample. We never went hungry.

Winter brought cold weather. A time to make sure you had plenty of wood and coal on hand for heat. The animals were kept in the barn and bedded for warmth with straw, water, and feed. The water cups had to be kept thawed. Without sufficient water, the milk production would drop.

The snow just kept falling and kept the town road crew busy. One year, my father was the road superintendent. The storms kept him working day and night to keep everything plowed out and moving. There was not much time for sleep. Winters were hard, but spring always comes!

MY FIRST PAIR OF ROLLER SKATES

My memory escapes me as to how old I was, but I was a young child. My big dream was to own a pair of roller skates.

My neighbor girlfriend had a pair of them, and I thought what fun it would be to skate with her instead of taking turns. She was always willing to share with me.

I finally devised a plan that would provide the money for my dream—the pair of skates. In those days, we butchered our own animals on the farm and cut the meat up and canned it for our meat supply. The animal not only had edible meat but fat and tallow. It was after the Depression, and the local grocery store was a collection point for fresh tried-out lard. Thus, it was that I would place the fat and tallow into large kettles on the woodstove to render coffee cans full of the liquid fat or lard.

My father would take this to the store for me and bring the money back. I believe I was paid ten cents for each coffee can full. The money was slow in coming, but when I got up to about two dollars' worth, Mom and Dad suddenly decided it was time to buy the skates.

They brought them home to me. I was overjoyed! There was just one problem. I really didn't have any place to skate. The milking was in progress, so no skating on the barn floor. The weather was cold and rainy, so one could not be outside. The problem was solved by my parents. They gave permission, and that evening, I skated 'round and 'round the dining room table!

Skating did continue to be one of my pleasures through high school. On one occasion in seventh grade, I was at a class party. We were in Wellsville, and I was skating with the principal's son.

Someone came around the corner, tripped us up, and we went flying. My partner headed to the hospital with a broken arm.

All through high school, I made sure I was on the bus when it departed for the roller skating rink. What fun it was!

OUR SCHOOL BUS

*E*ach school day at 8:15 a.m., we kept a close watch for the yellow bus to appear over the nob in the road. We could not keep it waiting! With only one bathroom and so many to share it, we really had to be alert.

Our bus driver was my aunt Adah's father, James Dunham, or my uncle Dorr Harrington. There were times when some of the children would misbehave. Suddenly, the brakes were applied, and the bus would come to a quick stop. The lunch pails slid forward on the metal floor, making a terrible noise. Jim, the driver, would then give instructions. It went something like this: "Sit down and shut up!" Everyone did as he said, and we continued our journey to school.

The Troupsburg Central School, where we attended, was built in 1936. Previous to that, the students walked or rode by horse-drawn sleds to the closest country school. Troupsburg still did not have a kindergarten. Upon becoming five years old, each student would attend first grade the following September. We enjoyed knowing all the neighbor children who rode the "Young Hickory Route."

We arrived home at 4:00 p.m. Sometimes Mom would have homemade bread just warm from the oven. Everyone would enjoy a slice. Now it was time to get the cows, feed all the livestock, and prepare the evening meal.

A good radio program, homework, or a softball game in the yard finished off our day. But before we knew it, it was time to watch for the yellow school bus coming over the nob again.

SCHOOL DAYS AT
TROUPSBURG CENTRAL!

*T*urning five, I went directly to first grade. Mrs. Matson was my teacher, and there I met my best school friend Arnet. We became long-lasting friends. She enjoyed visiting my home on the farm, and I was invited to her home in town often. We were cheerleaders together. She lost her father just after eighth grade while we were on summer break. I remember sitting alongside Arnet at the funeral and sobbing as I felt so bad for her. It was a difficult time and caused her family to have to move to another town so her mom could find work when we entered high school. Time and place separated us, but we always managed to get together, and our friendship has continued.

My first playmate and dear friend on the Young Hickory farm had been Chrystal. Chrystal and I enjoyed playing together. She owned a bicycle, dolls and a carriage, roller skates, and we colored. She was always so generous, kind, and anxious to share. She loved coming to my home when allowed. She was one grade ahead of me in school. If our moms wouldn't let us visit each other at our homes, it wouldn't keep us apart. We would meet halfway under a small tree and color together. Later in life, I introduced Arnet and Chrystal. As adults, they have become very good friends. We are all in our eighties, and the three of us love to get together and enjoy old pictures, memories, and good food. What a blessing!

Up through the grades, I moved. During my junior high years, I became a cheerleader. I also enjoyed playing on a girls' basketball team. I remember in high school doing well in a speaking contest. I was in home economics until high school. At the time, I was sewing skirts to wear with colorful grain sacks. I washed the fabric, and each bag was two yards, just enough to make a new skirt. I was delighted when my dad brought home a new bag of a different color. I could sew a gathered skirt with a fitted waistband that hooked on the side in two hours. My aunt was known to make her curtains from the grain bags also. There were so many of us, and money didn't allow for fabric from a department store.

Most of our entertainment was at school. The boys played basketball and baseball; class dances were held each month. Once a year, a nickel show with white elephant and other booths. Used items were donated and sold cheaply. A play was put on annually by the senior class. The school would run a bus on each route so everyone, including parents, could attend activities like the nickel show and the special trip to the county fair just before school started in the fall.

Each month during high school, a dance was held in our gym. I always seemed to have a date and stayed on the floor, dancing every dance. What fun that was. There were only fifteen members in our class. We were all good friends, and as high school seniors, we enjoyed a spring trip to Washington, DC, together. Our principal drove the school bus, and a male teacher and the school nurse accompanied us as chaperones.

During the course of two summers, when I was fourteen and fifteen years old, I worked in the house at a farm where they grew and sold fresh strawberries. I watched three children and helped cook. The day upon arrival, I was asked to read a storybook to a five-year-old boy. This young man turned out to become a well-respected medical doctor in the area who treated me later in life for heart problems.

So many happy memories!

THE BARN IS ON FIRE!

*I*t was the early fall of 1944. Dinner was over, and evening chores were done. There was a good movie on at the Westfield theater. Dad was planning to take the appropriate-aged children to see a movie.

All of a sudden, we heard someone call out, "The barn is on fire!" The fire company was called, but by the time they arrived, the barn was a total loss. We still had our animals: about twenty cows, two horses, and some young cattle.

A neighbor that lived down on the main road, approximately two miles from us, had a large barn, and Dad was given permission to house the cattle there for the winter. When the winter storms would come, Dad left our car down at the barn and came home with horses and a sled. Early in the morning, he hitched the horses to the barn sled and headed down the road with a thermos of hot coffee and lunch pail in hand. The older boys, Larry, Earl, and Roy, also went to help with the milking, feeding, and cleaning of the barn.

The barn had burned in September 1944. When the barn burned, there was an organized fire company. They wet down our house, which had been built with asbestos siding thus, it did not burn too! That same year, a B-17 crashed on a nearby farm. The plane was flying so low over Troupsburg that a young boy from the Roger's family thought the Germans had come to bomb us. Two soldiers jumped out of that plane over Uncle Roy's farm, causing their death. So they say, the sheer impact of their bodies hitting the barnyard caused their legs to burrow several feet deep. One soldier, the pilot, rode the plane to the ground and survived. Later on, in 1952, my family moved to the farm where the plane crashed.

Dad often worked at other jobs. He could manage doing odd jobs in the middle of the day. After evening chores were done, we watched down the road for his horse-drawn sled to appear. When he was in town, Dad purchased what groceries we needed: a pound of butter, four long loaves of Stroehmann's white bread, a box of Kellogg's corn flakes and Nabisco shredded wheat, a head of cabbage, a big can of Maxwell House coffee, and a few other items.

In the springtime, a new barn with a rounded roof took shape. Dad's father, my grandpa Bliss, had taught Dad how to build barns. The cattle were brought home, and eventually, life got back to what we thought was normal.

Following the birth of my brother Alan, Mom had surgery on the veins in her legs. This required ten days in the hospital and bed rest when she arrived home. They carried her in and put her to bed. I remember the shock of seeing Mom unable to walk. By then, I was a big helper. Dad's sister Aunt Mollie and her daughter, Joyce, came to help cook. After the evening meal, she would settle into her chair in the living room with a crossword puzzle or good book. My cousin and I did the dishes while the boys did the barn chores.

During her stay, my younger brother, Melvin, whom we all called "Jr.," soiled his pants. Aunt Mollie spanked him with a switch. Later that day, she went to the milk house, and while she was there, the boys locked her in. They crawled up on the roof to hear her begging before they let her out. We were so very glad when Mom was able to be Mom again!

Children and Getting Away

Even though I was raised a middle child in a large family and was a child myself, I helped care for my siblings. Therefore, I didn't have a full appreciation of the amazing things children are able to comprehend and say and do at an early age.

As an adult, I stand in awe just how much a little cuddled-up baby develops in just one year, their first noises, coos, smiles, those first teeth and how those teeth hurt, sitting up alone, creeping, climbing up, and all of a sudden, walking. Then they are off and running into everything. I must have done a lot of watching and protecting the younger ones. Pictures show they were always huddling around me. One of my younger sisters said to me jokingly as an adult, "The next time you button my coat, I wish you would button it straight!" My reply was, "I think it was buttoned crooked because some buttons were missing." She was noticing how she looked in pictures and agreed that was probably the reason. I remember hanging many diapers on the clothesline to dry in all kinds of weather. I certainly knew how to change them.

Because nursing was in vogue, my mother was the one to feed them. She loved babies and welcomed each one with joy when they arrived. She spent a lot of her life in front of the kitchen range, preparing wonderful meals or canning peaches, meat, and vegetables for the long winter months. Much of the time, we did not have a phone, so her social life outside the farm was minimal. She and Dad would go to the fair and watch the horse races or to a movie. They would invite another couple to go with them.

We never had a babysitter. The oldest one was left in charge the few hours they were away. We just seemed to go on with our lives and do what we were expected to do.

There were not many restaurants at that time. They were happy with a Texas Hot or an ice-cream cone. I am sure that was all they could afford anyway. A ticket to the Westfield, Pennsylvania, theater only cost fifty cents when I was a teen. Three or four gallons of gasoline could be purchased for about one dollar, and they pumped it for you. However, the car and gas were for necessity, and the times were few and far between they'd have a chance to get away.

OUT INTO THE WORLD

*L*arry was the oldest and the first to graduate from high school. "Gopher" never attended college. Bright, though, he was! After graduating, there seemed to be only one choice for him. He joined the Army.

It was a hot summer day when up the dirt road came that green Army car. Larry got in, and we watched it go out of sight. Mom sat with a pan of yellow beans on her lap. As she snapped them, the tears ran down her cheeks. Dad was working on a load of hay down at our uncle Dorr's farm. My uncle shared how Dad took out his handkerchief and wiped his eyes as the green Army car passed by.

There were happy times when Larry came home on furlough. One day, Mom was mopping the kitchen floor. She looked out to see Dad coming back from town. Behold, Larry got out of the car! Mom let out a yell, dropped her mop, and ran to the back door to greet him.

Larry went overseas to Japan. He served his time, came home, married, and had a son. Then he was called back to serve in the Korean War. When he returned home from Korea, his second son was six months old. He had been gone for fifteen months. His young wife had to go through the entire pregnancy and delivery before he was released to return home. She lived with us, and we helped with the two boys until his return from the Korean War. This made home a lively place!

My older sister, Betty, graduated from high school when she was sixteen. A new minister came to town to preach at the Methodist Church. At that time, there was a large active youth group. They came to our house for hayrides and hot dogs. Well, the new minister knew that Betty was one special lady. In the summer of 1946, a wedding took place. She became a beautiful bride and a pastor's wife. The reception was held at Grandma and Grandpa Harrington's house.

Betty and I used to do the dishes together—she washed, and I dried. She always said that it was the job of the dryer to get anything the washer missed! Now being the oldest girl at home, I got to do both! How I missed her.

Large families make their own fun! We grew up quickly and moved on with marriage and our lives. The eleven weddings were all different but beautifully planned as each couple desired. The best part was meeting and welcoming new ones into our family.

Soon to follow would be new babies. All unique and beautiful. Dad and Mom ended up with eleven children, but the days ahead brought many grandchildren and great-grandchildren. Along with tears came much delight.

Just a ball and bat and four large stones, and the fun would begin. There were always enough people to have two teams. I don't remember any anger or fights, but we all played to win. Younger ones were included and were encouraged. Much fun and laugher made for a memorable time.

Dad was great with barbecuing chicken. He would order one-half a broiler each. Mom stirred up the sauce, which came from a Cornell book, along with a large yellow Pyrex bowl of her famous potato salad and baked beans. The treat was unmatched and so-o-o good!

We all stuffed ourselves outside on a warm summer night.

NOTHING STAYS THE SAME

Earl worked very hard as all the boys did. He bought a milk truck and had a route to run twice a day. Before school, he went from farm to farm and picked up the cans of milk. Then he drove to Elkland to the milk-processing plant, unloaded the milk, and hurried back to school. After school, he returned the cans to the farmers before milking time. Roy took the milk route when needed. Over the years, Roy, Arling, Bill, and Alan all got that call early in the morning: "Get up! It's time to milk!" The boys were all good ballplayers and played on the school basketball and baseball teams. They also played instruments in the school band.

Earl fell in love with his music teacher, and she with him. A while after high school graduation, they were married. Virginia taught music, and Earl was employed at the leather company in which at the time was the largest leather tannery in the world. Earl was good at figuring out how to repair the old equipment. He liked and understood tanning and later became an owner of tanneries.

Roy went into farming. He also drove big trucks on road construction. He married Eileen. She became a school secretary and also did the payroll there for many years.

I was a senior at the age of sixteen. In early October, just two weeks after the birth of Bonnie, Dad came home for the noon meal and announced we were moving that afternoon. This was the first we had heard about it! He used the two available milk trucks to accommodate our belongings, and we left the Young Hickory farm. We moved to a farm down on the main road near the town of Troupsburg. This was the same farm where the B17 had crashed years before. The house was older, but with the help of paint and paper, it became home to us. What a day that was! Mom sent me along with the first loads to supervise the placement of our belongings and to prepare supper down at the new place. She stayed at the Young Hickory place to see that everything got packed and loaded and to care for our newest family addition. Bonnie was only two weeks old. This was not your average well-planned move, but it happened anyway.

One sunny spring day before my senior year, I was cleaning the family car. I chose to be outdoors by myself because I was expecting someone who would soon arrive to meet me that afternoon. My brother-in-law Jim had met and talked with someone he formerly knew from his hometown, Whitesville. I was informed to watch for a visitor, and he informed his acquaintance (Don Chase) that I was about to graduate and would be an available date!

Don did come, and we took a ride while getting acquainted. When we returned, he wanted to meet the family. I guess he was interested and liked what he saw. My parents invited him to stay for dinner.

ALAN'S BIRTHDAY PARTY

*I*t was getting time for my youngest brother's birthday. He was in the sixth grade at school, and he wanted a party. He kept saying that he was going to have a birthday party. Apparently, no one took it seriously because with so many children, birthday parties with more than one guest just didn't happen. His day came and no plans had been made at home. When the school bus arrived home that night, sixteen of Alan's classmates—boys and girls—got off the bus with him. Mom must have been in shock!

She called Larry, the eldest son. He was preparing to leave to work the second shift. He went into action and found a ride to work, thus leaving his car at Mom's place. Another brother, Bill, happily drove the car to town to buy hot dogs, rolls, and other items while Mom prepared a birthday cake.

The children enjoyed playing kickball, entertaining themselves in the yard.

It was a good thing Alan was born in the month of June, and there was no rain that day. One friend told Alan "that was the best birthday party he had ever been to!"

CHURCH

As a child, I just knew from nature that God was real. The flowers, the sky, return of spring, and the seasons. None of that could have happened without a God. When I responded to the altar call that I will write about in the next part, it changed things. I had a personal relationship with Him. My eyes were opened to what the scriptures were saying and what was within its pages for me. It brought happiness and joy.

Previous to that, I liked being in church and singing the hymns. When I asked to go to church, my dad would drop me off and pick me up. He waited during that hour at the town garage, spending time with the owner and his friend. When I entered the church, Aunt Rena (Grandpa Harrington's sister) would be standing there, singing from her hymnal. She held it down so I could sing with her. Mom and Dad found it too difficult to get all of us children ready and down to church.

As a child, one moonlight evening, Dad, Mom, and I attended a special meeting at the Methodist Church. At the end of the meeting, Dad went forward for spiritual help while Mom and I waited for him. Dad used to walk to the Baptist Church down the road a couple of miles from the Bliss homestead when he was growing up and some after their marriage.

Mom wrote how she got her parents to attend church at the Methodist Church on Mother's Day one year. That was the beginning of her family attending.

Through the years, as the family grew, Mom and Dad encouraged our attendance at summer Bible school, and when teens, the older ones had a wonderful group of friends at church in the youth group. Occasionally, someone would choose to go to summer camp.

After we were all married with families of our own, one year, Mom was selected by the church to be honored on Mother's Day. As many of our family as could attend appeared at our local church in town to celebrate our mother. We filled the whole center section. Everyone brought lots of food, and a beautifully decorated cake was ordered for this special occasion. All enjoyed a meal together in the church fellowship hall right after church. Mom was absolutely gleaming that day!

Oh Lord—It Hurts!

So with you: Now is your time of grief, but I will
see you again and you will rejoice, and no one
will take away your joy.

—John 16:22

What was your most difficult, painful experience in life? It may
have been war, divorce, surgery, and loss of loved ones. It might
be having a child. Our family felt the pain when the oldest son
left to serve in the Korean War and when brother Arling left after
graduation to serve in the Air Force. Years would pass in between
home furloughs.

Jesus promises us that after the pain, joy will be returned to us,
and He will rejoice with us in Spirit.

Jesus suffered the pain of being crucified, but the day of glory
and victory came when he arose again. He promised the disciples to
have faith, believe, and your joy will return, and it did! Have hope. A
day of rejoicing is coming!

Ask and you will receive and your joy will be
complete. (John 16:24 King James, NIV)

My Adventure

 $\mathcal{D}$ on was finishing up his degree in industrial arts at Buffalo State. Because of his desire to be with me, he drove to my home about every three weeks so we could date. In June, when I turned seventeen, I graduated from high school. In September, I went to live with my sister Betty and husband, Jim, while training to become a beautician. It was arranged that I would work for my room and board. I ran the vacuum cleaner and did laundry to help my sister with her responsibilities of raising three children. Every weekday, I would answer the alarm at 6:30 a.m., prepare myself for the day, have a small dish of cereal, and catch the city bus out front of their home. It required a forty-minute ride. I arrived at the downtown city library and was still ten blocks from the school! With no money to pay for the city bus, I walked the rest of the way to arrive and begin my nine-to-four school day. That gave me one-half hour to walk the ten blocks back again to ride the 4:30 p.m. return bus. I would arrive home at about 5:30 p.m.

One evening, I attended a special church service. When the pastor was done with his message, I went forward to answer the altar call. From that day forward, I knew I wanted to follow the Lord and His will for my life. The next evening, my future husband, Donald Chase, attended the service with me, and he also gave his life over to Christ. We dated through this time, and after being granted my parents' permission on Thanksgiving Day in November that year, he placed a diamond on my finger. I said yes! My parents had asked him to wait until I finished school to marry. The requirement for my state license was one thousand hours, which I completed on schedule in about seven months. By then, it was April, and my mother encouraged me to seek employment in Elmira, New York, at a penthouse beauty shop called "The Donald of the Ritz." I was interviewed and hired on the same day! I found a room to rent within walking distance, purchased my own food, and cooked for myself. Meanwhile, Don Chase is patiently waiting to marry me according to my parents' wishes.

About eight weeks later after turning eighteen, I became his wife. We were married at my hometown Methodist Church. It was a June evening candlelight service. My beautiful satin gown had been sewn by a wonderful and dear friend from the Boston, New York church. Since there were so many relatives, we held the reception at the Troupsburg Central School. This was a common choice at the time. Our honeymoon was a short trip around the northern part of New York State. Don and I then returned to Buffalo to finish his bachelor's degree, and I worked in a local beauty shop. After college, Don was hired as an industrial arts teacher at Kenmore Junior High. Over the summer, we began attending the First Methodist Church on Delaware Avenue in Buffalo. This is where we first met Marilyn and Larry who became very dear friends. We found spiritual growth through service and fellowship with several young couples. The pastor and his wife treated us just like their children. We helped them all we could when needed. It was a very happy time in our lives. People automatically loved my husband, Don Chase. He was one of the kindest men you would ever meet—very gentle and a real witness for the Lord.

As we came to know the Lord better and early on in our marriage, my husband, Don Chase, discovered his talent to sing. He had been blessed with a beautiful tenor voice. On the weekend, we would go to visit the parents and attend church. At that time, everyone at home was regularly attending and enjoying church. Don would render a solo. This always was encouraged and appreciated by the congregation. In time, spiritual growth came to all of us through our search for the living Savior.

He began to sing at many services and weddings. The following September, Don began his teaching career at Kenmore Junior High School. He sang in the Youth Time Choir in Downtown Buffalo. We were both in some of their musicals.

In 1957, our first child, Gregory, was born. Fourteen months later in April, our daughter, Valorie, joined our family. They kept my life busy and fulfilled!

While I was feeding Valorie one day, Greg decided to bring her box of dry rice cereal to me with the box open. Every step he took left a trail on the freshly vacuumed carpet! When Valorie got older, the two of them decided their riding horse needed a rub down of peanut butter. I suppose it felt gooey and good as they rubbed it on. They wiped their hands on the wallpaper of the apartment too. I tried to clean it. The landlady was very kind (although, I'm certain, not happy about it). We just left it that way until we moved.

Don loved his children dearly. We decided to move someplace where we could afford a house for our growing family. There was an opening for a teaching position for industrial arts in Bolivar, which is near Wellsville, New York. This was also closer to both our parents. We moved to Bolivar in the summer of 1959.

At the same time, Don began sensing the Lord calling him to pastoral ministry. He worked with leaders in the United Methodist Church, and in the 1960 Olean Conference, he became appointed to serve three churches in northern New York State beginning in the summer of 1960.

However, in the spring, Don began to act differently. He developed terrible headaches. In late June, near the end of the school year, we went to see the doctor. Don was diagnosed with a malignant brain tumor. He spent two weeks at Strong Memorial Hospital in Rochester. They operated on him, but sadly, they were unable to remove his cancer as it was intermingled throughout the brain. After returning to his room following surgery, the doctor's reports were not good. As evening approached, they brought a food tray of clear liquids for his dinner. As I spoon-fed him some broth and Jell-O and he sipped ginger ale, I teased him about his "fancy hat"—in reality, a head wrapped tightly with white gauze. One minute he was smiling at me, and the next he drifted into a coma and never woke up.

As the hours passed that evening at the hospital, I went with Phyllis, the wife of Don's cousin Lennie, to the chapel to pray. The situation was so dire concerning my husband's condition. Would he live? If he did live, what would he be like? I had just one short prayer. "Thy will be done." At that moment, I just gave it all over to the Lord. It was one of the hardest prayers I have ever prayed.

At midnight, the doctors insisted that I go home to rest. Marilyn, my friend from Buffalo, was a nurse and came purposely to special Don so I would leave the hospital for a short respite. Home was to be a cot in Lennie and Phyllis's kitchen. They lived in a two-bedroom duplex. My husband's parents were there also and bedded down on the living room sofa. At 3:00 a.m., the phone rang. My father-in-law answered the call. I was in a very deep sleep—so much so that I could not get up to answer it. During my sleep, just before the phone call, I experienced a wrenching pain. It felt like flesh being ripped away from my chest. I moaned out loud. My mother-in-law heard me and called out, "Audrey, are you all right?" To this day, I believe that it was at the moment of my pain that my husband died. We rushed to the hospital as they instructed in the call, but he was gone. Marilyn was with my husband when he died.

As I looked out the window at the hospital, I thought, "Dear Lord, I am too young to be a widow! I am just twenty-four years old with two small children, two and three years old. They need their daddy! Are they old enough to remember him? Lord, why?" Then it came. Peace. Flowing like a river. God was so real. I felt him holding me in the palm of his hand and saying, "Don't be afraid. I will take care of you and your children." Then my mind flooded with the scripture that had been my husband's verses to live by. "Trust in the Lord with all your heart. Lean not on your own understanding; in all your ways acknowledge Him, and He shall direct your paths" (Prov. 3:5–6 NKJV).

We all pulled ourselves together, best we could, and left the hospital for the two-and-a-half-hour trip to my parents' home. I knew my three-year-old son and toddler daughter were waiting there for me. When we arrived, I took my son by the hand, and we walked out by the big maple tree with a swing. I told him that his daddy had died.

He looked at me and said, "Why did my daddy have to die?"

I explained that "Daddy had become very sick and that he had gone to live with Jesus."

I felt the awful hurt that I knew my son was feeling. Later, as Mom and I were collecting Don's clothing for the funeral home, Greg was there with another question. We had laid out a shirt and tie, a suit, and other items, but we hadn't put out shoes.

He asked, "Do they wear shoes in heaven?"

God did take care of my children and me. He brought many wonderful things into my life. He was my friend and my guide. We had been married for six years, and this loss was incredibly sad and hard. But my faith carried me through.

I was invited to stay and live with my mom and dad. This would provide help for me with the children and stability for all of us. There were three siblings still living at home, brothers Jr. and Alan and sister Bonnie. I did not try to work outside the home. I felt the children needed me to be right there with them, and my mom needed assistance, not more children to care for. I needed time to grieve.

Audrey's Photos

Dad's Parents

Richard & Florence Stiles Bliss

Mom's Family

From top left: Mildred (Mom), Fannie (Grandma),
William (Grandpa) Roy, Door, Craig

From top left: William & Fannie
Center: Dorr, Mildred Bottom: Craig, Roy

A Time of War and Rations

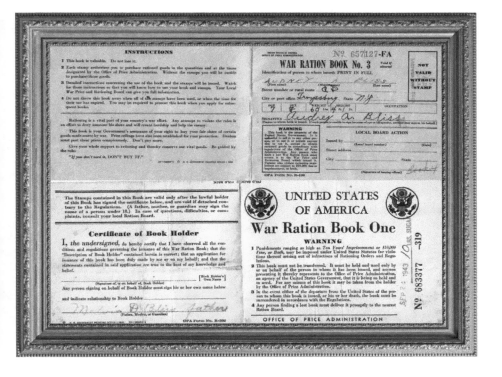

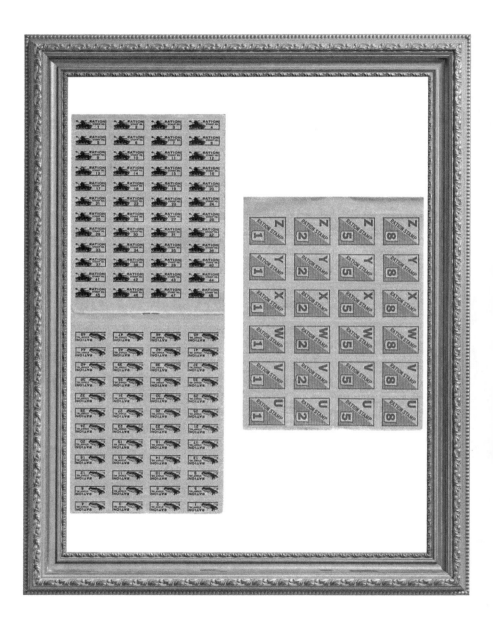

Uncle Craig Harrington

The School Bus

Young Hickory Bus—Jim Dunham (Driver)
Chrystal is white dress dark socks 2nd to left from me!

The Children

From left: Arling, Audrey, Roy, Earl, Betty, Larry
(taken in front of the house that burned)

The Granary & the farm my parents Built.

More Babies To Come

From back left: Audrey, Arling, Bill Melvin Jr., Cousin Marie, Judy

Ten and Eleven

~The Family is Complete~

Alan

Bonnie & Mom

Betty Bliss Graves Wedding Day—July 1946

From top left: Betty & Grandma (Fannie) Harrington
Center: Audrey
Front Left: Mom (Mildred Bliss) with Judy on her lap
Front Right: Aunt Adah Harrington with Marie on her lap

Mr. and Mrs. Melvin D. Bliss
request the honour of your presence
at the marriage of their daughter

Audrey Ann

to

Mr. Donald Keith Chase

on Monday, the twenty-first of June
nineteen hundred and fifty-four
at eight o'clock

Methodist Church
Troupsburg, New York

August 1956

Mildred (Mom & Dad) Melvin

From Back Left: Audrey, Mom, Judy, Bill,
Melvin Jr & Dad, Alan & Bonnie

Greg & Valorie (taken by Don Chase)

GOD'S PLAN—A NEW DON

*I*n February of the following winter, I received a call from Jr.'s agriculture teacher at school. He invited me to go bowling. After just three dates, Don Brotzman wanted to meet the children. Yes, another teacher named Don! As he put it, "I am getting very serious about you." By the middle of April, Don bought a diamond for me, and in June 1961, we were married.

Well, the first year of marriage was a rough ride! Don Brotzman was an only child with two elderly ailing parents, and I was a widow with two preschool children. In addition to teaching full-time, he was working on his master's degree at Alfred University. Our honeymoon year included me coming down with scarlet fever and all three of his new family needing tonsillectomies. I repeat, the first year was a rough ride!

In May 1963, baby Steven joined our family. It was difficult after the delivery as I had an infection, and it went into the baby's lungs. I asked the doctor three times if the baby was all right. Just after the third, I thankfully heard him cry. The doctor had been suctioning Steven's lungs. They put him in an incubator, took him away, and I didn't see him until the next day. Overnight, my infection broke. As my parents sat with me the following day, the doctor told them he'd been very concerned in the night and was happy to see their daughter that morning! I don't think he was certain if I would make it through.

So now we had three children. The oldest, Greg, had started kindergarten. Daughter Valorie was anxious to go when she turned five. Baby Steven had colic and cried a fair amount. The situation was hard for Valorie. The new baby was getting way too much attention, and she missed her older brother Greg. She treasured the time when big brother came home from school.

Don finished his master's, and he accepted a guidance counseling position at a high school near Rochester, New York. We purchased a home in nearby Churchville. The lawn was knee-high with hay, and the faded gray shingles complemented the faded pink shutters. There were hardwood floors throughout, but each room needed to be scrubbed and painted. Nonetheless, it was quite a step up from our apartment over the grocery store. This seven-year-old split-level became home. The children found new friends, and we settled in. We had many exceptional friends in our neighborhood and church during our years there. Many years later, they are still our friends.

THE BLIZZARD OF 1966

On a Sunday evening in late January 1966, my husband, Don, and oldest son, Greg, came back into the house. They had been shoveling the driveway as a big snowstorm was in progress.

Don said, "You might as well know, we are snowed in!"

This was our normal winter protocol for this time of year, but what made this statement interesting was that I was two weeks from delivery with our fourth family member. My oldest daughter had been born two weeks early, and our son three weeks early. To say I was apprehensive would be an understatement!

The neighbors started calling to tell Don to get me out of there. They didn't have a detailed plan for us, and one jokingly said, "Don't call us if Audrey goes into labor!" One kind neighbor at the end of our street remarked that she had some experience and said she would come. Having had farm experience, Don joked that "I've delivered several calves." Needless to say, I went to bed anxious, afraid that labor would start.

That storm turned into a full-blown blizzard! For several days, we were snowed in. On Greg's ninth birthday, we celebrated by making homemade cards with things at home. Each contained handwritten messages and poems. We enjoyed spaghetti by candlelight and finished with a birthday cake. Though he was disappointed that his local friend, David, couldn't join us due to the weather, Greg's birthday party was a fun and memorable one for our family.

Don had called the doctor and the town roadmen to make them aware of our situation during the storm, and they would have tried to respond if we had needed them. The storm continued for a few more days and then stopped as suddenly as it had started. The sun came out, and the snowplows went into action. They headed our way, and we were among the first to be plowed out.

The road edged high with banks of snow. Don and I headed for the hospital. That evening, our fourth and last child, a beautiful baby girl, whom we named Carla, was born. Carla arrived on President Lincoln's birthday.

When she was just a toddler, one Saturday morning, Don awoke in great pain. The diagnosis: rheumatoid arthritis. Little did we know then just how the disease would make a huge impact on our lives. It would become acute and then subside in remission. The joints were wearing out. With much determination, he managed to work until he retired as a teacher at fifty-five.

Don worked very consistently to improve his educational status. He got his master's and then continued to be accredited to be a guidance counselor as well as a high school principal. He had graduated from Cornell University as an agriculture teacher. He always took his jobs seriously and worked very hard at them. He had committed his heart to the Lord, and he helped at church also.

Our children were good students and hard workers. As they grew, they kept the lawn neatly mowed and helped me around the house. They worked for neighbors by doing farmwork and babysitting. All four graduated from high school and obtained college degrees. We were very proud of them and all they accomplished.

HELP CAME AGAIN
THROUGH FRIENDS

*W*hen Carla was just a toddler, she decided she wanted to just drink milk and chew on her bottle rather than show any interest in real food. She acted like she was ill and short of breath. We had a new doctor in town, and four weeks in a row, I took her to him for help. She cried much. He treated her with penicillin, but she was getting worse. Something was very wrong. I went to the grocery store to buy some items and met up with a friend who was married to a pediatrician named Dr. Darling. She asked me how things were, so I told her how concerned I was for my ill daughter Carla.

She said to me, "Go into the store and get what you need. As soon as you return home, call Dr. Darling's office, and you will see him today!" I did as she said, all the while thanking the Lord for help. Dr. Darling found an infection and with blood tests discovered how low her red blood count was. Her count was one-third of what was normal. How thankful I was for the help. From that day forward, he was our doctor for all four children. What a wonderful Christian family they were! How thankful I was for the Lord's timing.

DEPRESSION

*D*on eventually took a position as an Ag Teacher in the southern tier. We relocated to a country home in Jasper and then several years later to a home closer to town in Canisteo. While living there, I experienced a clinical depression. My regular doctor suggested I enter the hospital for treatment. Eventually, I did go, signed myself in, and stayed for two weeks. The hospital in Sayre, Pennsylvania, had a wonderful program to participate in, and I saw my doctor every day.

I learned a lot about living a balanced life (some work, some fun). I met many new friends and came out of there feeling wonderful! I had been given a very low dosage of medication. The doctor said he felt I was exhausted when I entered. The right program and the rest found me well again. I am grateful I was able to go.

It is very hard when you are feeling so depressed and to be willing to admit just how bad you feel. I thought I could or should be able to pull my own self out of it by trusting the Lord at a deeper level.

When you are depressed and down, your body and thought processes are ill. You need the right doctor who can guide you to unloading the hurts and disappointments in your life. To have a plan with not only work but fun things of enjoyment to be part of. You need balance in your life.

Loneliness was a big factor too. Find happy things that please you to intermingle with the work demands. There is room for you in this world, and it needs your contributions of joy to encourage others. You are not alone. Jesus became my closest friend.

He can guide our way to answers to our needs. They were at the wit's end. They cried out to the Lord in their trouble and He brought them out of their distress. (Ps. 107:27–28 NIV)

A Growing Family

$\mathcal{W}$e had some beautiful church weddings. Greg married Jackie, Valorie wed Marty, Steve married Annette, and Carla wed Tom. We were so glad to have new family, and these were special times in our lives.

The grandchildren started to arrive until there were eleven: Andrew, Daniel, Lindsay, Marty, Jordan, Valorie, Philip, David, Vanessa, Joseph, and Benjamin. The grandchildren were so special. I tried to stay close to them and help their moms and dads when I could. In addition to being a grandma, I also became a full-time caregiver for Don during these years.

Through the years we had with our children and grandchildren, it was very important to me to teach them about Jesus and how He wanted to live in their hearts. I wanted them to know Him as their closest friend and helper but also to know the joy of serving Christ by helping others. As Don and I passed through all the rough days of surgery and sickness, we felt the Lord's presence so real in our lives. I will share some of those times in the following pages.

ONE HUNDRED DOLLARS

*C*hristmas was soon approaching. The Sunday evening church service was over, and as I left, I found myself conversing with another Christian lady. She and her husband had three teenage children. She always had a smile and a willing heart to do the Lord's work.

We were discussing Christmas, and I asked if she had completed gift shopping. She quietly shared with me that they could not buy family gifts for each other on that particular year because their income had been cut. She already babysat to bring in more income.

Upon arriving at home, I shared our conversation with my husband, Don Brotzman. His immediate response was what I had hoped for. He said, "Make out a check for one hundred dollars and mail it tomorrow." As Christmas was one week away, I was delighted and did so.

A few days later, I received a phone call from her. She said she had a story to share. It seems that she had a niece who was going on a mission trip. Many people were giving freely to her niece to make this trip possible. Her son had come home from school, feeling a bit disgruntled. He did not think his cousin was really deserving of what people were doing for her. He was not sure about God. He made the statement "No one ever sent us one hundred dollars."

She swiftly moved to obtain our letter with the check that had arrived that day. She handed it to her son. His eyes grew large, and his faith was renewed. God's timing had been perfect.

That was enough of God's goodness, but the story does not end there. They all received their twenty dollars, and each decided upon and purchase the personal gift of their choice.

Now she was a very talented person, so she chose a book of craft patterns. From this book, she made lovely things and entered a craft show. People liked her work and purchased the items. Seeing her success, her close friend took advantage of her and copied her work. The other woman became the competition. She knew that she needed to get a patent to keep this from happening, but how could she? The cost would be four hundred dollars.

At that time, it was brought to her attention that they were having a drawing at the craft show. The prize was to be four hundred dollars cash. She was not sure that it was right to buy a one-dollar ticket for a chance to win. Others knew of this. Without knowing, someone entered her name. Sure enough, the name was drawn, and much to her surprise, she had won!

If you see crafts marked with the name Elegant Elly, you will know the rest of the story!

Her business venture and hard work was a large boost to their financial situation. The whole family did so much work for the Lord.

MANY ANSWERED PRAYERS

After retiring from teaching after thirty-two years, Don began having joint replacement surgeries to replace his worn-out joints. One by one, hips, knees, shoulders, finger joints, wrists, ankles, double hernia, lung, and arthritic cysts on his elbows—a total of twenty-eight surgeries in his lifetime. At one point, there were four surgeries in a row, one every six months. Life was a huge challenge.

It was early October. As I was doing my housework and thinking about yet another surgery to come, I began to pray, "Lord, Don will be in the hospital for surgery and recovery for ten days. He enjoys seeing the fall leaves when they are in full color. Would it be possible for him to get a private room with a window so that he could enjoy the view?"

On the morning of surgery, we arrived at the hospital at 5:30 a.m. We were told to go to admissions because a problem had arisen. Though our insurance only allowed for a semiprivate room, all those rooms were full. The woman that was doing the entry asked if a private room would be okay, though we would only be charged for a semiprivate one. We assured them it would be! As we entered the hall, I told Don of my earlier prayer and how this was a direct answer. I could not wait to see the room! I hurried to the window to open the curtains. It was a beautiful view! It was all there—a schoolhouse nestled on a hill surrounded with brilliant color-laden trees. Visitors to Don's room would ask, "How did you get such a beautiful room?" We could say that it was a direct answer to prayer! Reservations were made with the heavenly hosts.

On another occasion, I had not prayed specifically for extra help. Don was having surgery: the patella was replaced in his left knee, and his right ankle joint rebuilt. His recovery would require no weight-bearing pressure and a wheelchair. I was concerned about how I would manage his care and, more specifically, how I would transfer him once home.

Friends from our church in Rochester were in Sayre, Pennsylvania, where the hospital was located. They were in town for a relative's funeral. As nurses were placing Don in the car to go home, they pulled up and parked right behind us! They followed us home, and I was not alone. How humbled we were by God's gracious care of every detail! After settling in at home to recover, caregiving became a challenge. Don at six feet tall and 190 pounds and I at five and a half feet made for some pretty interesting days. For a long month, I bathed him and changed the sheets, all while he was still in bed. Our son Steven would come in the middle of the day to help with getting him up. We would move the wheelchair close to the bed, and with the help of a therapy belt around his waist, Steve would wrap his arms around Don, and he and I would pivot Don into the wheelchair. Steve later observed that these were some of the last hugs he ever gave his father. We enjoyed lunch at the table together and then back to bed for him!

One day, a phone call came from our friend. She wondered if their daughter could live with us while she attended college nearby during the winter semester to finish her degree. Knowing that God was providing for us, we agreed to have her stay with us. It was then that we learned that she was training to become a physical therapist! She came from college each day at dinnertime and put Don in the wheelchair and brought him to the table. She and I shared after dinnertime doing dishes, and then she would sit with the retired teacher-patient and share all that she was learning. He was so interested and engaged with their conversations. What a blessing she truly was to help us through this time. Only the Lord could provide for us in such a wonderful and unexpected way.

God's Provision in Time of Need

*I*n October of 1993, we enjoyed a vacation with our good friends, Pat and Steve, in Myrtle Beach, South Carolina. As we headed home, we stopped for an overnight hotel stay.

Don took a shower, but when he bent over to dry his feet, the hip socket prosthesis popped out of its place. Suddenly, one leg was four inches shorter than the other. He cried out in pain. The three of us were able to get him seated on the bed near the telephone. He called the hospital where he had endured several joint replacement surgeries. He was desperate to find out what to do. An emergency room nurse answered his call, and he asked for the orthopedic surgeon on duty.

"Who was your doctor?" the nurse asked.

When Don answered "Dr. Cohen," she replied, "Dr. Cohen is right here in the emergency area," and she handed him the phone. It was after nine thirty on a Sunday evening.

What assurance we had that things would work out. Dr. Cohen advised that Don needed transport to a local hospital by ambulance. Imagine our surprise when he also let us know that there was a good orthopedic surgeon there as well! Again, God had provided for our every need.

While waiting for the ambulance, a lens fell out of my glasses. Many years earlier, after my mother-in-law's passing in 1966, I had found a repair kit for glasses in Don's mother's handbag. Thinking that someday I might need that, I slid it into my purse. Now all these years later, without a lens in my glasses to see, how would I fix them? Steve used the repair kit, and in less than ten minutes, the ambulance had arrived, and I could see again. The hospital was just five minutes away.

After arriving, I began reading and signing forms so that Don could receive treatment. How would I have done any of it without my glasses? Another need that God had supplied! The orthopedic surgeon arrived within a half hour, and with X-rays taken, Don was on his way for treatment. Medicated in the ER, the doctor attempted to pull on the shorter leg in hopes of putting the hip back into its socket. Too tight to cooperate, the joint required surgery. Don was taken up to the operating room.

Just then, a nurse came down the hall and apologized. She had wanted to pray with Don before he went to the operating room. The Lord had placed her there at just the right time for us. While in the waiting room, an Amish couple was also waiting beside us. They were there awaiting news on their critically ill grandson, and they were sharing how prayers had been answered in their lives. Though burdened, they set an atmosphere of peace and calm, trusting in the Lord. At 2:00 a.m., the surgeon returned with a big smile. Don's hip was back in its socket without surgery, and he would be discharged the next afternoon! We headed back to the hotel for some much-needed sleep, thanking God for all His goodness to us during our unexpected ordeal.

When the anesthesiologist came to visit him the next day, he revealed that Don had been an anesthesiologist's nightmare! Due to spinal cysts, he would require a neck brace to immobilize him during potential surgery. Additionally, he had come to the hospital with a full stomach, and he had just had recent surgery before this had happened. Thank God, Don didn't require an operation, and he was doing just fine.

When we left the hospital at three thirty the next afternoon, we were told that Don would need a walker when we arrived home six hours later. He was anxious about where we would get one on such short notice. I tried to console him. "Don't worry. Something will work out." I prayed for the first three hours of our trip.

We stopped at a McDonald's, and I made a phone call to our son in New York. When our daughter-in-law answered, I told her what had happened and named some people from our church who might have one and also the local Lions Club. Greg, our son, had a friend who was active in the local Lions Club in town. One call to him, and a walker was delivered to our doorstep. Greg had a key to our house, and when we arrived at 9:00 p.m., the living room light was on, the house was warm, and a walker sat just inside the front door.

It was a moment when tears came. The look on Don's face was worth a million dollars. I had not told him of the phone call to Greg because I didn't want to get his hopes up in case it didn't work out. Within five minutes, Don was safely in bed at home. "Before they call, I will answer; while they are still speaking, I will hear" (Isa. 65:24 NIV).

Thanks be to God for all His provisions for our needs and the wonderful support from family and friends.

MOM'S BIRTHDAY

The long-awaited June 17 had arrived. Today was Mom's eighty-seventh birthday. Four sisters were traveling from their homes to spend this special day with Mom and each other.

Betty, the eldest, lived on Wauneta Lake in a lovely trailer during the summer months. She placed her gifts for everyone and Mom's carrot birthday cake into her car and drove one hour to Troupsburg, the town where Mom had spent her whole life. Betty was the first to arrive.

Meanwhile, the other three sisters were loading their gifts and dish of food to share into their cars. Audrey lived in Churchville, near Rochester. Audrey had a fresh fruit salad, plus a flat dress box for Mom and three wrapped shoeboxes holding the gifts for her sisters. She traveled for two hours and was the second to arrive.

Judy, the next in age, had left Syracuse, where she lived, at 9:00 a.m. She had prepared angel-hair pasta with seafood. Her gifts were all alike in shape. Four long stem rose boxes from the florist shop. What could possibly be inside? Judy had the longest drive of three hours. She arrived at 11:50 a.m., the last to arrive.

Bonnie, the youngest sister and baby of the family of eleven children, had made a one-hour trip from Watkins Glen, arriving about eleven fifteen. Bonnie had four square wrapped boxes. She had remembered to buy bows and paper, and they all matched. Her fresh rolls and large tray of meats and cheeses completed the meal.

The coffee was prepared, and the colorful plates and napkins were placed on the table for the noontime luncheon. Mom, the honored guest, offered the prayer of thankfulness. The food was passed, and conversation was plenty.

At 1:30 p.m., everyone cleared the table of dirty dishes and put away the food. Each found a comfortable chair, and the sharing of gifts began. Judy gave each one of the long boxes and instructed us to open them all at once. We all lifted a beautiful doll from our box. Each doll was very similar but different and unique. Oohs and aahs were to be heard around the room!

Soon Betty was passing gifts to each one. Mom received a ring and a light-blue knit top, decorated with flowers. Audrey's gift from Betty was a two-cup teapot. Very dainty and pretty, Judy's present was a small chest, holding three basket drawers, and for Bonnie, a floral overnight case.

Bonnie was now sharing the square boxes with all. Mom and Audrey received a Hallmark teacup and saucer.

Now it was my turn to share gifts. For Mom, I had purchased a short-sleeved top with royal-blue knit slacks. Bonnie, Betty, and Judy opened the shoeboxes. From the boxes, they took their handmade wooden dolls. Each crafted with love by me, adorned with soft lifelike hair, and dressed differently for each sister. The sisters wondered how Audrey had kept a straight face when the first dolls were opened.

Mom now shared her gift and envelope containing a card and a fifty-dollar bill. What special gift will we purchase with this money? It must be carefully chosen—something to keep.

The clock did not slow down. After more sharing and laughter, it was time for each to head out to their own homes and responsibilities. A special day of memories had been made once more.

Happy birthday, Mom! We did it another time and hoped for next year to do it again.

My Quiet Spot

*I*t may have been 1:00 or 2:00 a.m. I had just awakened from what I had hoped would be a restful night's sleep. The house was quiet. Only a dim light made the furniture in the room form shadowed shapes. There were some other shapes—the shapes of a wheelchair, a walker, and all the other paraphernalia from surgery recovery. Things that provided assistance and entertainment filled the room. The TV, VCR, and other electronics cast their own shadows, taking up any remaining floor space. Don was asleep, sporting an open toe cast that went up to his knee. The cast had been his companion for four months.

I found myself tossing and turning. Sleep did not come. I needed to get out to my quiet spot in the living room near the large bay window. I looked out before moving to the couch. The shapes of the houses, trees, and mailboxes were all so clearly visible. All was quiet. All were at rest…except me.

As I went to lie down on the couch, I reached for my large hand-knit afghan. My niece Lucille had given it to me. Her custom was to pray for the person she was giving it to while she knit. So it became my "prayer blanket." Once wrapped in the warmth and comfort beneath my special blanket, I began to pray. God's peace settled over me and within me. When I opened my eyes, morning had come.

Life kept busy with Don's surgeries and recuperation periods. They helped to keep him mobile and lessened his pain for several years. The stubborn ankle joint that had been operated on refused to heal, even after two separate surgeries. He was fitted with a customized removable cast. He could walk with the cast, but once it was removed at night, he would need help or a wheelchair. Getting him into and out of the shower became a daily challenge. At 10:00 p.m., we would finish the process of drying between each toe. I silently talked to the Lord, asking, "How long can I do this?" I was growing so physically tired. The Lord would answer, "Wash my feet." To me, he was saying, "Keep taking care of Don and trust me." It was not just a struggle for me. For Don to be a good patient and keep in good spirits was a huge job for him. A verse that daily encouraged my faith was "Be strong and of good courage; be not afraid, neither be thou dismayed: for the Lord thy God is with thee wherever thou goest" (Josh. 1:9 KJV).

After what was to be his last surgery for a while, Don arrived home with a new knee joint. The surgery was a great success and homecare was going very well. Suddenly, Don became so very ill, unable to eat, and ran a temperature. He grew worse and worse. I prepared his favorite meal—meatloaf and mashed potatoes—thinking it might help to get his appetite back. Instead, we ended up at Strong Memorial Hospital. The children were always so faithful to be there when needed. I called Greg, and we sat in the emergency room at Strong until 3:00 a.m. The medical staff had completed diagnostic tests and admitted Don. During the next twenty days, tests were done and redone. Don would become very ill and then rebound. Without any concrete diagnosis, mid-April, the decision was made to do exploratory surgery to attempt to save his life. At 10:00 p.m., two doctors appeared from the operating room. They explained that they had found a huge intestinal mass and that it was cancerous. They said they had never seen anything like it. After surgery, Don remained on the respirator. He was kept comfortable during the night, and we were told to stay close by. He could hear us and would respond by moving his toes. We took turns during the night by his side.

His health-care proxy gave instructions that he was not to be kept on the respirator. We knew that when they took away the respirator, he would die.

Early the next morning, we were told to go get breakfast in the hospital cafeteria. When we returned, they asked for my signature to remove the respirator. Forty minutes later, Don entered eternity. How he went through and handled so much surgery and pain, I could not fathom. Surely the Lord gave the strength for the days. He was sixty-three years old. Now he was free from pain. Signing the proxy for the removal of the respirator was heart-wrenching. I did it, but I surely did not want to.

At the age of sixty-two, I was a widow again. It was different this time than at twenty-four with two young children. They were my purpose each day as they bounded out of bed, full of energy. Don and I had weathered through twenty-eight surgeries. I had fed him, bathed him, and met his physical needs. His last hospital stay lasted twenty days. Back and forth I went from the hospital, home again to sleep, and back again. My whole life had revolved around him and his care. Now all that was over.

Somehow, the children and I went home. I called the undertaker and muddled through the day. I groaned in pain and found myself carrying Don's dirty T-shirt around with me, the one that I had brought home from the hospital. The children took turns calling relatives and friends.

David and Vanessa, two of my grandchildren, were there to greet me with their happy child smiles. I knew life would go on, but it would be so different. I would be living alone in a four-bedroom house with over an acre of lawn to mow. In that moment of his death, *my* whole life had changed.

The day of his funeral, the weather was wet and cold. As we said our goodbyes at his grave, the cold rain was biting into our faces. It was brutal. We returned to Churchville for yet another memorial service to be held at our church on Sunday afternoon. Many people came to honor Don and support our family. He loved people and had shown a real interest in so many lives, actively praying for many of them. Each one's show of sympathy and caring was deeply appreciated.

Our youngest daughter, Carla, stayed with me that first night and returned to her home and family the next day. Now I was alone with the empty house, the empty chair, and the empty bed. I prayed and asked the Lord to be with me, to help me not be afraid, and to help me sleep. Sometimes I would awake in the night to the mournful sound of the passing train's horn, echoing in the darkness. I cried and moaned but would eventually be blessed with sleep. I was not afraid.

My prayers had been answered. Now it was time to rest, grieve, and eventually, with the Lord's help, figure out my future.

In the evenings, I would try to watch TV but couldn't stay focused and would end up falling asleep. My exhaustion was catching up to me. All the paperwork began to come in the mail from the hospital stays and health insurance. Don also left a car in his name to be given to our son, who lived in Pennsylvania. Many trips to the DMV and a rainy trip into the city courthouse, and finally, that was settled. Life was moving on and taking me with it. To what, I did not know.

Please Meet Us for Lunch

When Don and I lived in Canisteo, New York, we attended the Free Methodist Church in Hornell. We became very good friends with Pastor Mike Stepanian and his wife, Donna. We worked hard together, ministering to the people in that church. After Mike and Donna moved to another church, we stayed friends, getting together for lunch every now and then.

Years later, after Mike and Donna had moved to Buffalo to minister, Donna became ill. She was fighting stomach cancer. They called Don and me to invite us to join them for lunch in Batavia, New York. During lunch, they shared that Donna had been told she had three months to live.

This was such sad news for us. I cried off, and on for two days, trying to wrap my mind around losing one of my best friends. Donna fought hard and lived fifteen months. I had no idea at the time that Don would precede her in death. Now, in early June 1999, Don was already in heaven, and Donna asked me to visit her in my own grief. My friend Sue drove me to Buffalo to see Donna. This was our last time together. Her last words to me were, "Be there for Mike. You are the only one who will truly understand what he is feeling."

While I was still grieving and adjusting to life without Don, Mike entered the picture. He was also grieving the loss of Donna, his wife, my good friend, but his mind told him, "I have got to go see Audrey."

Mike and I began to talk on the phone about once a week. We shared our pain, our hurts, and our sorrow. One day, Mike asked me to meet him for lunch. We met, retracing our steps at the same restaurant where the four of us had last met. Now, it was just the two of us. It was a hard time missing our spouses together.

Mike asked for permission to visit me at my home. When he visited, we took a lot of walks up to the nearby water tower, sharing our hurts and concerns. He was definitely interested in a future with me, but I was holding back. I would not even hold his hand. In my living room, in front of the bay window, we sat side by side in the fireside chairs and shared in the afternoon sunshine.

I thought to myself, *Is it too soon?* I needed more time to grieve and write and do things I enjoyed. I needed to find myself. I told my children that I was not interested in another marriage. I had been through two and lost both husbands at the same Strong Memorial hospital to cancer. I had become very independent. And then, one day, Mike asked me if I had any interest in him, romantically. My reply was, "Unless I truly fall in love again and the Lord shows me that it is the thing to do, I probably would leave things as they were."

THE LETTER

The first Christmas after Don died, I received a letter from my big brother, Larry; a timely word of encouragement and even guidance.

Dear Sister,

Once again, the season is upon us, and in a flash, it will be behind us. Forty-nine years ago, during Christmas week, I got off a ship in Inchon Harbor and walked toward the tracer lights of shells and the sound of battle. Many men died that night while the temperature dropped to forty degrees below zero. Many froze their hands and feet. God kept me out of harm's way at that time, and he still is. Praise God! Therefore, Christmas should be a happy time. Have a Merry Christmas and a Happy New Year.

With love,
Larry

PS: I'm glad that you have a friend at this time in your life. You can draw strength from each other. And again, I say, God will take care of us.

ANOTHER WEDDING

$\mathcal{S}$omething was happening. Through all our afternoon times of sharing and processing our grief together, Mike and I were growing close. I knew I didn't want a marriage of convenience. I told him I would pray about it.

One day, while alone in my home, thoughts were coming to me. It was like God was saying to me, "What is wrong with you? It's all right. Go for it!" I could hardly wait to see Mike again. I was falling in love again! I felt so alive and young. I was so happy, and life seemed to be beginning all over again. When Mike asked me to marry him, my answer was yes. Our love grew, and our marriage followed.

It was hard on our children. There had been so many adjustments for them. They did not fight it though, and we were able to have a beautiful family wedding, with everyone there taking part. By the year Mike and I wed, my dad had passed, but Mom was able to attend. She shopped with me and chose a long blue flowered dress to wear. My youngest brother Alan and his wife, Kathy, provided the transportation for her to attend. We shared communion with all that attended during the service, and Mom was unable to leave her seat to receive it, so our bishop served her in her seat! She told me afterward how special that was for her to have Bishop Snyder perform that kindness. Mike's son, Michael, who served in the Air Force, and his daughter, Denise, and her family (adding two more grandsons, Brian and Chase) were all a part as well. Bishop Snyder and Pastor Brown led us through our vows with Dave Anderson at the piano, and Ted Roy singing in full tenor voice, "Great Is Thy Faithfulness."

In late June, after our wedding, Mike and I began an interim pastorate at the Free Methodist Church in Warsaw, New York. We had a wonderful year—serving, grieving, and laughing together. Mike and I served two more churches before the end of his career. We moved into retirement together and enjoyed serving wherever the Lord led us.

Serving together was a wonderful experience. Mike couldn't give enough to the Lord. He had a big heart! One day, we came out of the grocery store to see a man struggling to get his car started. We had jumper cables, so we took the time to help him. It was a cold day, and the man did not even have a coat on. Yep, you guessed it! Mike took off his coat and insisted the man was to wear it and keep it. We had no idea of his name, or who he was. What a joy to know and serve the Lord!

> But now this is what the Lord says, "Fear not, for I have redeemed you; I have called you by name; you are mine. When you pass through the waters, I will be with you; and when you pass through the rivers, they will not sweep over you. When you walk through the fire, you will not be burned; the flames will not set you ablaze. For I am the Lord your God; the holy one of Israel, your Savior." (Isaiah 43:1–3)

Mike became very attached to Carla and Tom's second child, Ben. Being he was the first grandchild born after we were married, Mike was there, waited through his birth and held him. They just seemed to bond. During this time, I was spending a considerable amount of time getting to know Mike's grandsons, Brian and Chase, as they spent weekends with us.

Over the years, one after another, the great grandchildren came. Val and Marty's grandchildren—Heiress, Joey, Jayden, Chase, Kaden, Deklyn, and miracle baby, Chandler. Greg and Jackie's grandchildren—Logan, Lily, and Elsie Joy. Each with special and unique characteristics and behavior. All beautiful children. All loved very much. It is amazing to watch them grow and witness the pleasure of their parents when we spend time together.

HORNELL

$\mathcal{M}$ike and I moved to Hornell in our retirement because my mom had to be placed in a nursing home as she could no longer walk. My brother Roy and wife, Eileen, had been seeing to her needs but were becoming weary in doing so. Thus, we moved close by to be able to fill that role for her care and to see her often.

Shortly after that time, Mike's father, "Papa," called to see if he could come to live with us. He was ninety-two by then and had been living with Mike's brother Bob in North Carolina. Mike told him yes!

Soon after that, my brother Earl was diagnosed with Alzheimer's disease. His wife, Virginia, was older also and not managing the situation very well. We saw the need and, with much help from the rest of the family, moved them to Hornell into the house right next door to us. We managed his care there for eighteen months and, then because he was wandering, placed him in a nursing home.

The time, I was allowed with Mom was brief as she passed shortly before Earl and Virginia ever arrived in Hornell. However, there was still a need for us to be there! After Earl's death, Virginia continued living near to us for two more years. Mike and I, with the help and kindness of others, continued providing care for her through that time. Virginia's nephew was to see to her care when she was no longer able to live alone. She was then placed in a nursing home near Corning.

Papa, out for a walk one day, fell and injured his spinal cord. He only survived overnight.

It was much caregiving, and the Lord gave us the strength to handle the responsibility. He carried us through it all!

ALL IS NOT WELL

Before Mike's retirement, by his own admission, he had developed an addiction to prescription painkillers. A doctor in Buffalo had given him his first prescription to help with back pain. X-rays showed Mike's back had deteriorated greatly. He had progressive, degenerative arthritis of the spine. His dependence on the pain medication, including OxyContin, which was supposedly nonaddictive, slowly grew. As years went by, his dosages of these medicines slowly increased. Mike never once took a medicine that wasn't prescribed to him by a doctor, but he was becoming an addict.

We coped with this addiction for about ten years. Mike's behavior was, at times, difficult to deal with. It was a very hard thing for the entire family. Relationships were tested. Support is so critical, but others didn't understand, and friends and family became silent.

Finally, when we were living in Hornell, I told a local doctor about Mike's problem. He decided to not give Mike any more medicines and apparently decided to go on vacation. I was told that he would need to go through withdrawal in the hospital. I knew that Mike would not go for that because we feared they would put him in some sort of a locked unit, and he was claustrophobic. We lived two blocks from the hospital, so we decided to stay at home with him and watched him closely. Mike and I decided he would go "cold turkey." I knew that this was against medical advice: he might go into seizures. He might die! But we could not go on as we were. Things had to change. A very caring pharmacist helped us choose a nonaddictive pain medication, and though it was a very challenging process to go through, we prayed for the strength to get through it. Withdrawal took weeks, not days. Each day, Mike made progress. Once his system cleared, we had "Mike" back again.

After our experience, I noticed newspaper articles and TV news reports about the prescription drug addiction crisis in our country. Mike's experience is happening all over this country. Who knows how many people out there are suffering from this very thing? Once we got through it, we found that relationships healed, and life was getting better. We decided to move to Chili Center, New York, in the suburbs of Rochester. There, we rented a lovely two-bedroom upstairs apartment. We were very happy there.

HERE WE GO AGAIN!

$\mathcal{S}$oon after Mike recovered from drug addiction, Alzheimer's disease was moving in. It wasn't long before I began to notice behavior changes. He remained the same sweet guy, but he was becoming more confused. Finally, after a visit to the doctor, an MRI revealed a lesion on his brain. For the next two years, we thought he was suffering from a brain tumor. A new doctor ordered a brain scan. The results showed that a large portion of his brain had advanced Alzheimer's disease.

"Lord! Is this really happening? I've already said goodbye to two husbands. How can this be?" Mike and I went out to lunch at the Acropolis Restaurant. As we stood at the cash register to pay the owner, he wanted an update on Mike's health. By the time I had gotten through that, I headed to our car and threw my arms around Mike and cried. Reality had hit!

"I am going to lose you, Mike," I said.

He sadly said, "Let's go home," which we did. Once there, he walked up behind me, put his arm around my waist, and said, "Let's get married!"

Since we had already been married seventeen years at that point in our lives, it really was sad. That is what Alzheimer's disease does to people's lives. Slowly, day by day, you lose your loved one.

Family support is so important. All my children were supportive and promised to do whatever they could to get us through it. That meant so much to both of us.

As his condition deteriorated, he began to sleep for longer periods at a time. Here is some of the writing I did as he slept,

> As I write, the dark clouds of anguish have cast
> their shadows on my life again. Seventeen years

ago, I married a mentally sharp, well-dressed man—a minister of the gospel. His greatest desire was to serve his flock and bring others to the knowledge of Christ. Even though his memory is fading and his sharpness waning, his greatest desire remains, to serve.

Life is hard for him now. He struggles to maintain. One moment, he is very clear, and the next, someone completely unknown appears. He is lonely and wanting fellowship. Some days, I am his dearest one, and others, a threat, making him irritated and unsure. He needs several naps to keep his spirits and strength lifted.

He is missing his son, who is deployed in Iraq. He should be able to be home soon, and hopefully, this will ease his mind. He has said, "I'll be mad as hell if I die before he gets home."

His brother and wife live in North Carolina and plan to come for a visit for his birthday. It has been a couple of years since he has seen them. They have come to know the Lord and his goodness, so we have much to share.

Mike sleeps often, and sometimes he just sits at his desk and holds his head. He says he has nothing to do. He still takes pride in his appearance and enjoys going out for breakfast or lunch. He always leaves great tips for the waitresses but gets confused when it is time to count money or pay the bill. Life is definitely not the same. The illness is taking over.

As his Alzheimer's disease progressed, we knew that our upstairs apartment living situation required changes. Things were getting much harder. We moved to an assisted living facility nearby so that when he wandered or fell out of bed, I would have help. We lived there for ten months until Mike's death in July.

In Mike's final days, he stayed very good-natured and sweet. Many times a day, I hugged him and told him I loved him. Even when other words would no longer come to him, he would look at me with his beautiful brown eyes, and he could still say, "I love you very much." He was neat and good-looking with his well-trimmed beard and mustache. One afternoon, two days before his death, he rose in bed to a sitting position with both hands toward heaven. He said, "It is time. It is time." He was seeing something not visible to me. It was just a day or so later when he lay very still and, quietly and peacefully, left for heaven.

It was a good decision to move to the assisted living facility and stay with him until the end. It gave us more time together, and even though it was sad and difficult, it was memorable and comforting to be with him. We had nineteen years together. The workers and staff were loving and caring. We met many wonderful people. They came into our room to visit and share. We even had a visit from Santa! They were all professional and kept a faithful eye at the front desk. They helped admit us with ease and keep us comfortable. We had numerous helpers and especially enjoyed our table friends! Everyone was so kind, including those who kept the painting done and cleaned faithfully every day. Many thanks to all of you for your caring and loving ways!

I am so glad that I could be there for the care and love Mike needed to get through his final days. It was very hard, and my loss feels big, but that is the way it needed to be.

Now I am learning a new life without him. I am excited to have use of a kitchen again as I have always taken great pride and enjoyment in preparing food, eating, and feeding family and friends. I tend to my own housework of three rooms, do my own laundry, take walks, and care for house plants and the porch and garden flowers. I have daily devotions and treasure this time spent reading my Bible and praying for others and their needs.

When I take my daily walk, I pass by two lilac trees in the yard. Now that spring is here, the deep purple buds are opening, and they are sending out their aroma. It brings a reminder of my loss, and tears come as lilacs were Mike's very favorite flower.

I am so thankful for happy memories and that I can still remember!

Mother's Day 2020

One of my favorite times in life was when each child was born. Such a tender, overwhelming joy! When you become a mother and are so busy keeping your child diapered and fed, it is a delight that tires the mind and tests the body and our patience. As time passes on and more children arrive, you can become quite worn and weary. A mother takes on the challenge of keeping up with the demands and needs of motherhood. Breaks were needed, money was short, so simple answers had to fill the need.

I am so grateful that I could experience being the mother of my four children and step mother of Mike's son and daughter. This year, at the ripe old age of eighty-four, I still received much recognition from them. I received two different outfits to expand my wardrobe, beautiful roses, and my bathroom accessories redone in my favorite color. Wow! So much!

The thing that surprised me was the thoughtfulness also from grandchildren. I received a miniature red rose bush to be planted, cards with special handwritten notes, and phone calls of thanks and praise.

When you are a widow and older, sometimes you feel just in the way, but anyway, "thank you" for remembering me on Mother's Day! I truly felt celebrated and appreciated!

The Honesty and Humor
of Children and the Joys
of Grandchildren

When I had the privilege to work with a class of fifteen four-year-olds in a Christian nursery school, I appreciated their open and complete honesty.

One day, a local doctor's daughter came into class, sat in her chair at the play table, and said to me, "My daddy has diarrhea."

Another day, the son of another local doctor joined our class. He informed me that his mom would not go into their attic because they had mice in their attic!

How I enjoyed having grandchildren. Andy was spending some time with me one day. Often, he would perch on the counter next to where I was working. This particular day, he was hoping for cookies. One of his favorites was Fig Newtons. He said, "Grandma, have you got any more of those 'fig noodles'?"

Andy kept asking each day if this was the day he could go to school. All summer, he kept asking. Finally, that day arrived, and off to school he went. By the second or third day, he had decided he did not like going to school. It was a long year for his mom getting him to attend.

Brother Dan started kindergarten a bit later. The first day, a boy wanted to fight with him. His report of it was "He wanted to fit, so I fit him!"

Dan was sitting on the counter as Andy always did. Dan wanted to know what "A—Number One" meant. His Grandpa would always say that to him. I explained to him that "A—Number One" was as good as it gets. That satisfied him.

Younger brother Jordan was in the hospital. His mom needed to go home to tend to the other children. She asked me to stay with Jordan. While there, being young and ill, I said, "Jordan, Grandma would like to give you a kiss, but I don't know where I can kiss you." Jordan pointed to his forehead and said, "Ma always kisses me right here." Thus, I did likewise.

Sister Lindsay was the third child born right between two boys older and then to come two boys younger. Dan was with me one day, and he had a real taste for homemade strawberry freezer jam. When I made it, I put it in old yogurt containers to freeze it. I gave Dan a container to take home with him, thinking everyone could enjoy a peanut butter and jelly sandwich. Lindsay later reported back to me about it. She said, "Grandma, do you know what Dan did? He took that jam up to his room and ate the whole thing by himself and did not share any of it with us." She was really angry with him!

I took Lindsay on a shopping trip for a really nice dress for her. Rather, she chose two simpler dresses that were less costly. She returned home very delighted!

When my daughter and son-in-law were in their early days of getting their semitrucking business built up, my son-in-law was a driver and required him to be away from home all week. Thus, my daughter was the office girl, plus raising five young children. In the evening, she would ask her family, "What would you enjoy doing special tonight?" It might just be a ride or maybe an ice-cream cone. Young Marty spoke up. He wanted to go visit "Looper!" She was a retired grade school teacher, and her real name was Marge Loper. The family had visited her before, and as a young child, that was his idea of something special to do. She probably had good treats, but Marty was a kind boy too. I believe they all enjoyed it, and knowing her, I am sure she did also.

Another grandson came to stay overnight.

Phil asked, "Grandma, can I 'pit' [spit] down the hole?"

Thinking he meant the drain, I said, "Yes, Phil, that would be good."

He was talking about the overflow hole when I realized what he meant!

Sister Valorie would come to stay and bring her friend Audrey. I prepared blueberry buttermilk pancakes for breakfast, or they would enjoy cereal in bowls of varied colors. When I became a pastor's wife, I had to produce some items to donate for a sale table. I made the mistake of donating the cereal bowls that she had thought were so very special. Valorie said, "Grandma, they were special to Phil and me!" She went to the table and bought the bowls back.

Joe, David, and Vanessa would come from a very small age to meet and play at Grandma's house. They delighted in playing train with three cardboard boxes.

When Joe would come by himself, we had old toy hockey sticks and a putt. At that time, we lived in a parsonage. That home had a large back room carpeted with indoor, outdoor carpet. It was great for a game of hockey. Joe was young and very competitive. Mike and I really had a lot of fun playing with Joe.

More memories come to me as I write, especially the time Joe, David, and Vanessa came for a visit. They decided to play hide-and-seek in our apartment. The problem was, there were not many good hiding places. Leave it to Vanessa—she thought of the perfect place behind our living room drapery. Even though quite young, she kept very still and silent. Joe and David spent several minutes hunting for her. She really "got their goat" as the old expression goes! She had outsmarted them by being so quiet.

Another fond memory about the oldest grandchild. Andy would spend some weekends with us and go to church with us. I got Andy ready as he was probably less than two years of age, and he headed for the carport. Carla stepped out the back door, Andy's first comment was "Nice day, Tarla!" Then he said, "You look nice, Tarla!"

Dan happened to answer the phone at their home in Jasper. Carla talked to him, "Dan, what are you doing this morning?" His reply was "Eatin' thereal!" Oh, a young child's voice and expression.

Jordan was saying his good night prayers with Mom listening. He said, "Dear God, I hope you are alive." Well, let me assure you, God is very real. Just talk to Him like your closest friend, and He will delight your soul.

When I met Brian (Mike's grandsons), he was about five in age, and Chase was in a stroller. While Mike's son and daughter were sorting out Mike's house before our marriage, I bathed Chase and rocked him to sleep. Brian asked if he could call me "Grandma." I told him "that would be perfect." He said he was cold and wanted to cuddle, which we did.

Grandchildren grow up and become wonderful help when painting, sorting, and moving.

Grandchildren are wonderful to have. How we enjoyed the children.

Now most of the great-grandchildren have arrived. They have started calling me Grandma Great because they already have a grandma.

Some verses from Deuteronomy:

> Impress the Commandments that I give you on your children. Talk about them when you sit at home and when you walk along the road and when you lie down and when you get up. (Deut. 6:7–8 NIV)

> Tie them a symbol on your hands and bind them on your foreheads. Write them on the doorframes of your houses and on your gates. (Deut. 6:9 NIV)

Today we could say, wear a Christian theme bracelet, a cross necklace, hang-framed pictures and sayings on your walls, also, maybe a cross, but let the world see that you love the Lord.

> Love the Lord your God with all your soul and with all your strength. Then the children will learn through the years and follow. (Deut. 6:5 NIV)

Children seem to understand our strengths and our weaknesses and are able to sort it out, remembering the good and laughing about the bad. They are smart and intuitive!

Family Life and Loss

*D*ad passed away in October when he was seventy-eight after a fall in the hospital that caused fluid on his brain. While in the hospital, he wished to go home to the green rolling hills. His eyes were as blue as the sky until his passing.

Mom stayed quiet and sweet while in the nursing home but died in December during a hospital stay with heart and physical problems. She died at the age of ninety-six, prior to losing any of her children.

Larry, the oldest son, came back from the Korean War to a wife and two sons. He went back to farming, and he and Evelyn had four daughters and one more son, making a total of seven children. Larry left the farm and went into construction. An extremely handsome and talented architect, he soon became a supervisor and oversaw the building of churches, college dorms, schools, and a huge mall. He divorced and remarried Dorothy, and they lived in South Carolina. Larry, after much wonderful care from Dorothy, passed away at age seventy-nine in the late stages of Alzheimer's disease on the same day and month he was born. Larry's first wife and first child have both passed away.

Betty, the oldest daughter, while married to the local minister, had two sons and one daughter. Betty followed Jim in the ministry to Oregon, where he abandoned her and the children. Betty worked in the hospital there and cared for her family. Eventually, she returned to New York and home. She lost her second born, a son, in a tractor accident when he was a young teen. She married again to a wonderful man named Leon. They enjoyed great food, fishing, and owned a great amount of land. After Leon passed away and retirement came, Betty cared for Uncle Craig and then moved to South Carolina. She loved to sing in her church choir and was a vital part of the church. She came back to New York to be close to her children and enjoy the many grandchildren. Eventually, age caught up with her, and she was wheelchair-bound and in a nursing home for several years before her death in January at age eighty-six. Her funeral was a wonderful tribute to a life well-lived.

Earl continued to excel in the tanning of leather and owned tanneries. He traveled extensively worldwide with his business dealings. Later in his career, he cowrote a book about leather tanning. Earl actually had a football and basketball branded with his name and gave them to the family. He and Virginia had one daughter. They lost beautiful Melody to cancer when she was fifty. He developed diabetes and died in the late stages of Alzheimer's disease in May at age seventy-seven. His talented wife, Virginia (an exceptional music teacher), passed away almost six years later. She had dementia. They had one grandson who was the "apple of their eye!"

Roy bought a different farm and retired from driving truck on road construction. He lived near Mom, and he and his wife, Eileen, carried much of the responsibility for her care and finances. Their first child, a son, died at birth. They had three beautiful daughters that love them beyond words. Roy died as good-natured as he lived his life with bone cancer in May at age seventy-three. Eileen passed away recently, almost one year after suffering a stroke. She handled her time of difficulty with great dignity.

Since I am next in line, I will tell you that I now live with my daughter and her husband not far at all from where I grew up. I have a small living room, bedroom, and bathroom to myself. I am trying to piece my life together and rest after having some health problems since Mike's death. I am active in the church, attend a Bible study, and have a chance to see my siblings, three other children, and their families from time to time. In addition to writing this book, I enjoy playing Scrabble, cooking and baking, and doing my own housework and laundry.

Arling joined the Air Force upon graduation from high school. He was stationed in France for about four years. When he returned, he brought his beautiful dark-haired Belgium bride into our family.

He attended college on the GI Bill to become a teacher. He was a talented carpenter like Dad; however, health issues have changed day-to-day activities for both of them. They had two sons and a daughter. They lost the oldest son very unexpectedly with a heart attack in his sleep. Arling is loved more than he will ever fully understand.

Bill married Dorie (the sister of Roy's wife). They decided to farm it! Eventually, he built a grocery store and worked it into a small restaurant. He was a good carpenter and an excellent cook with Dorie working especially hard right along with him. Business really boomed. He expanded the food service, making wonderful pies, cookies, subs, pizza, fish fries, and more. Dorie worked a job at another local business part of the time as well. They had two sons and a daughter. He built three houses for Dorie and one for each child before he passed away from a blood clot in November when he was age seventy-one. Heaven gained a wonderful musician as he could play the banjo like an angel on a harp.

Judy had five children with her first husband (two boys and three girls). She became a registered nurse. After their divorce, she married a man named Don and had two more girls for a total of seven. That marriage also ended in divorce but led her down the road to the love of her life, Joe! They live in Upstate New York, where they previously worked as counselors. They are good for each other, full of laughter and adventure while they age together and care for each other! Her son Todd died in a motorcycle accident at age forty, leaving a wife and two daughters.

Melvin (Jr.) attended a university in the south after graduation and became an agriculture teacher. He and his wife had a son and daughter and went through a divorce. He then remarried Carol and enjoyed many years with her and her five children until she died of lung cancer. Carol wrote a book about herself for her family. He retired after teaching for twenty-two years and drove the school bus. Through the school, he met his present and beautiful wife, Rose. They are happily married and keeping up with all their children. They live in Pennsylvania and enjoy family and travel.

Alan, the youngest son, married his beautiful and happy wife, Kathy, after attending technical college. He worked in air-conditioning for a while, then returned to college and obtained a math degree. He took a position as director of housing and oversaw negotiations for the construction of subsidized housing. They have been married for over fifty years and have a son and daughter. Their first grandson spends a great deal of time with them. He and Kathy retired from their jobs and are now pastoring at a church where Mike once served. Kathy also cares for her elderly mom. Alan still enjoys reminiscing about his years in sports, and they have worked hard together in their beautiful home. Kathy fills his heart and home with laughter.

Bonnie attended college and became a dental hygienist. She can light up a room with her sweet spirit and giggle. She married Denny from a family that had farmed in the area all their lives. They had a daughter and two sons. They moved from Pennsylvania and bought a grocery deli store, where they were very successful with sales and catering. The youngest son went west to study astronomy. It was there that he was shot and killed in a tragic event. Bonnie returned to college and became a paralegal and now works for a law firm. Denny now has MS and is at home in a wheelchair. He keeps a good attitude, and she is a wonderful caregiver. They also spend a great deal of time with their grandson who keeps a good eye on things, is a great help, and fills their life with joy.

Our family has experienced much loss, including that of my grandmother who died in the old farmhouse when it burned to the ground. Those we have lost will never be forgotten, but strength comes from within, and there is always a new joy to fill us and the desire to build our dreams.

Mr. & Mrs. Donald C. Brotzman—June 1961

Back: Greg & Valorie
Front: Carla & Steven

The Bliss Family

The Brotzman's

Audrey & Don
Greg, Steve, Carla, Valorie

The Weddings of Valorie and Greg

Valorie and Marty—1976

Greg and Jackie—1977

Our 25ᵀᴴ Anniversary

The Weddings of Steven and Carla

Steven and Annette—1988

Carla and Tom—1991

Our Trip to Myrtle Beach

Don & Audrey with dear friend Patty

Artwork from a greeting card(artist unknown)

The Greek word for "minister" is also the same for "servant"…
One who selflessly attends to the needs of others

Wash My Feet

Mr. & Mrs. Michael Stepanian

Fulfilling the Lord's Plan

Audrey Stepanian

Revelation Spoke to Me

Revelation Chapter 5
(King James Zondervan)

The apostle John wrote what was shown to him during his exile on the island of Patmos. May this enlighten our hearts and minds. May we see and understand more of who Jesus is.

John was told by the angels to write a scroll of what was shown to him. The scroll with writing on both sides. It goes further to ask the question, Who is worthy to break the seal and open the scroll? No one in heaven or on earth, except for the root of David. This being Jesus.

Chapter 5:6 says, "Then I saw a lamb who looked like it had been slain."

Jesus was from the house of David. He is the only one worthy because he was slain. With His blood, He purchased men for God from every tribe and language of people and nation. Verse 6 tells then he saw angels, numbering ten thousands upon ten thousands singing,

> Worthy is the lamb who was slain to receive power and wealth and wisdom and strength and honor and glory and praise forever and ever. Amen.

He has changed my life. He can change yours.
To God be the glory!

Handling Grief

- I personally wanted to face my loss and not run from it. With the Lord's help, I needed time to grieve and feel it—to pass through it.
- Move ahead with a positive attitude. A pity party is allowed, but remember, death is a part of life. Everyone will experience it.
- Plan something to do every day. Keep your home, mow your lawn, and pay your bills.
- Keep your habits. I went to church and sat where we used to sit.
- Let your tired body rest.
- Cry when you need to.
- Clean out the belongings of your loved one when you are ready and not before. I cleaned out my husband's clothing and donated them to the local mission.
- Share time with your extended family and friends. I made dinner weekly for my son's family.
- Pray together. I prayed through my husband's list of needs—even when he couldn't.
- Take time to have daily devotions. This gave me peace and strength for each new day.
- When invited to do something, I tried it. I didn't make excuses and stay in my safe world. Friends were very thoughtful and encouraging.
- Trust God. He showed me that His grace is sufficient.
- When you are ready, try to use your experience to encourage and bless others.

The words of a favorite old hymn come to mind:

> Trust in God through all your days. Fear not for
> he doth hold your hand. Though dark the way,
> still sing and praise, sometime, sometime, we'll
> understand.

- I found a book on grief, by Elf Help Books, Abbey Press
  Publications, very helpful.

SCRIPTURE

Jesus told Martha, "I am the resurrection and the life. He who believes in me will live even though he dies and whoever lives and believes will never die. Do you believe this?" Her reply, "Yes Lord I believe that you are the Christ, the son of God, whose was to come in to the world." (John 11:21–27 NIV Bible)

So many times through life, especially the illness and death, I have had to rely on the Lord for strength and understanding. When the hard things in life come to you, and they will, we need the assurance of God's Word. He provides that just at the right time. *He holds you by your right hand.* Many verses throughout the Bible were shown to me in these trying times, and I did feel his strength upholding me. I have listed them as follows:

Proverbs 17:22
Philippians 4:13
Isaiah 41:13
Isaiah 41:9
Isaiah 41:10
Isaiah 42:6
Zephaniah 3:6
Hebrews 14:14
Psalm 139:10

Your right hand upholds me. My soul clings to you. (Ps. 63:8)

Closing Thoughts

*A*s a child growing up, one of the middle children in a large family and with just the necessities of life, I had to stand on my own two feet and be creative and strong. Many things that seemed hard at the time eventually proved to be great blessings in my life. Those things prepared me for the things I would face later in life. By the time I was four or five years of age, I still have a sharp mental picture of much of the happenings in our lives. This was real to me. I watched the house burn. I lived it! It was a good life—happy but very difficult sometimes. That seems to be how life is. We have so much we have learned and so much to be thankful for. The Lord has carried us through. We all have a story!

When I gave my life to Jesus Christ, I found my identity in Him. I became His child and truly felt His love for me. In so many ways and so many times, as you have read, in those hard times, God showed me His love and grace. Provision came. Hope came…along with thankfulness as I anticipate each new day.

So many times as I spent time reading the Bible and devotional books, incredibly meaningful and appropriate for the moment verses would stand out to me. It was God's Word telling me, "I really will hold you by your right hand!" Many times at night, wide awake, unable to sleep, I would pray, holding up my right hand to the Lord. Comfort came. Sleep came.

So here I am. In my mind, I see myself as I always was, ready to whirl through each day, but my body won't keep up anymore. Therefore, I have become what you would consider an old lady now—and a widow again. I am learning to do less and rest more to adapt. Through the encouragement of others and my Lord, I have now shared my story. My hope and prayer is that my story will encourage you, bless you, and give you a renewed hope. To God be the glory!

For those struggling through the dark days and nights of hopelessness, the tears flowing and the feeling of anguish is very real. Maybe you are feeling very much like you have hit the wall and are so very alone. Trust me, there is someone who knows and cares.

As you read my story, may the Great Comforter reach into your heart and bring peace and a feeling that you will make it. Life will begin again, and you will find yourself smiling again and much richer for what you have experienced.

The Lord has carried me through each loss and period of grieving, restoring me each and every time. There is an old hymn that was a favorite of my dad's that comes to mind.

> On the Jericho Road,
> There is room for just two,
> Just Jesus and me.
> *There were three!*
> *And now there are two!*
> *Just Jesus and me.*

ACKNOWLEDGMENTS

A big "thank you" to my friends who were led to offer words of encouragement to me. God spoke to me through you. Many thanks and much appreciation go to my children. Without their help, this book could never have become a reality. Your dedication and encouragement have meant so much, and I love each one of you!

Many men outwardly look big and strong, but inside, they have meek, caring hearts and much gentleness. I believe the Lord knew I had the strength and ability to be there for the needs of three husbands. He brought them to me. I never had aspirations of being married three times, but I am very thankful. They taught me so much, and life was quite an adventure. It was trusting the Lord for each day. Now I'm doing it as a widow again.

RUN TO JESUS

Audrey Stepanian

April 5, 2020

Run to Jesus
God's precious only Son
He gave Him freely
Our souls to be won.
Dying on that cruel cross
If we Jesus do accept
We will gain life
Not suffer loss.
For our life He does give
Joy each day that we live
His word helps us to see
Life forever, eternally.

About the Author

An eighty-four-year-old Christian woman whose nature is to be both creative and speak the truth. Family and friends are very important to her. She delights in seeing them enjoy a home-cooked meal and just spending a happy time with each other. She likes to encourage people and share what she has to help others. She feels very blessed. The Lord has been her closest friend, seeing her through many challenging times. Writing is a positive outlet for her.

CPSIA information can be obtained
at www.ICGtesting.com
Printed in the USA
BVHW020744180721
612125BV00025B/428/J

9 781662 426407